DISCARD

Women in Sport

an annotated bibliography

and resource guide

1900–1990

Women in Sport

an annotated bibliography

and resource guide

1900–1990

MARY L. REMLEY

G.K. HALL & CO.

BOSTON • MASSACHUSETTS

First published 1991
by G.K. Hall & Co.
70 Lincoln Street
Boston, Massachusetts 02111

10 9 8 7 6 5 4 3 2 1

Library of Congress Cataloging-in-Publication Data

Remley, Mary L.
    Women in sport : an annotated bibliography and resource
guide, 1900-1990 / Mary L. Remley.
       p. cm.
    Includes indexes.
    ISBN 0-8161-8977-3
    1. Sports for women – Bibliography. I. Title.
Z7963.S6R45 1991
|GV709|
016.796'0194 – dc20   90-20557
                                    CIP

The paper used in this publication meets the minimum requirements of
American National Standard for Information Sciences – Permanence of
Paper for Printed Library Materials. ANSI Z39.48-1984.   ∞™
MANUFACTURED IN THE UNITED STATES OF AMERICA

To Rosina Koetting, who pointed me toward the paths "less travelled"
that have made all the difference.

And to the memory of my mother, Kate, who allowed me unusual
freedoms for a girl of the 1930s and 1940s,
my sister, Betty, who knew how to share her love,
and Eleanor Metheny, whose intellect challenged
many of us through the years.

Contents

The Author

Mary L. Remley holds a B.S. from Southeast Missouri State University, with majors in physical education and English, an M.Ed. from Ohio University, and a Ph.D. from the University of Southern California. She is professor of kinesiology and coordinator of graduate studies at Indiana University, Bloomington, and has teaching and research responsibilities in the area of sport history and women's sport history. She also serves as adjunct professor of women's studies.

Preface

Man's involvement in sport, games, exercise, and dance is as old as civilization. Throughout history the athletic prowess of man has been extolled or excoriated, depending upon the esteem in which physical activity was held. Literature through the ages has discussed the role of sport, play, and games in the life of man. Rarely, however, has much attention been given to the place of such activities in women's lives. Nonetheless, woman's involvement in sporting activities also has a heritage as old as civilization. Ancient Egyptian women played ball and performed acrobatics; Cretan women participated in bull dancing; Spartan women had their own version of the Olympic Games, the Heraean Games, in the fifth and sixth centuries B.C.; and medieval women rode horseback, danced, hunted, and learned to "carry the falcon gracefully." In the United States women's sporting heritage dates back to the establishment of the colonies. Early female settlers ran foot races; women of the mid-nineteenth century played croquet, bathed at the beach, and ice skated; late nineteenth-century women emerged as bloomer girls, bicyclists, and basketball players. Women of the twentieth century may be found in the gym and on the court or the field, playing all kinds of games, and competing at the highest levels of excellence.

Until recently, resources that offer insight into the female sport experience were fairly scarce. Although some sources were available in the nineteenth century, most have been published after 1900. Selections for this bibliography were made from materials printed since that year. Books offer, by far, the most comprehensive look at the development of sports for women, and every effort has been made to provide the broadest sampling possible. Relevant titles have been identified through searches of several computerized databases, noncomputerized card catalogs in the Library of Congress, and older issues of *Books in Print*. Several titles were found, by chance, in the stacks of the Library of Congress as I examined the titles discovered from other sources. With a few exceptions, the books are products of American publishers; most are available in academic libraries, and virtually all publications cited may be found in the Library of Congress. Some sources, published in England or Canada, have been included either because their subject matter is unusual or because they are commonly found in American libraries.

Books have been arranged in chronological order by year and then alphabetically by author rather than by subject heading, primarily because this arrangement provides an overview of the development of sport for women in the twentieth century. The dearth of publications in the early years of the century and the plethora in the last two decades indicate the increasing interest in women's activities. The assignment of years to chapters reflects my own view of important periods in the development of women's sports during this century.

Three sources of information other than books have been selected for the bibliography because of their specific relevance to women in sport. Periodicals that focus only on women's sports and those that devote more than sporadic attention to women's topics are included. With few exceptions, these publications are currently available. National sports organizations that are open to women's membership and those that are exclusively for women have been identified along with a mailing address and the major purpose of the organization. Halls of fame have been included because they are another indication of the growing interest in women's sports and provide a means of recognizing those women who have achieved success in the sports world. Each hall maintains some biographical information for those inducted. Dates of initial publication for periodicals and the establishing dates for halls of fame and sports organizations have been supplied for most entries, thus indicating time periods of developing interest in women's sporting activities. *Ulrich's Serials*, *The Encyclopedia of Organizations*, and *Sports Marketplace 1989* provided information about these sources.

Because of the ease of accessing information with present-day technology, dissertations and theses pertaining to women's sport have been omitted, and specific periodical articles have not been listed. For persons interested in these categories, the following databases may be helpful: Sport Discus, ERIC on CD ROM, Psychlit, Sociofile, and Medline for periodical information and Dissertation Abstracts Ondisc for theses and dissertations.

Every effort has been made to find the available resources concerned with women in sport; no doubt, many have been overlooked or have eluded me. I hope such oversights are not too numerous.

A major portion of the information provided in the book was developed from resources in the Library of Congress. Publishers, too, have been generous in supplying information upon request. Special thanks must go to a number of individuals without whom the completion of this task would have been considerably more difficult: Ada, in the HPER Library; Jo, Nancy, and Barb, whose hospitality helped make the Library of Congress stacks more accessible; Judy, who dealt with all the chores I neglected while sitting at the computer; and the editors at G. K. Hall, who were patient in the extreme as I neared completion of the project. I would be remiss if I failed to acknowledge the many students through the years whose interest in women in sport continually challenged me and whose probing questions demanded more than the status quo. They and the active sportswomen at all levels who continue to be the motivation for the growing body of literature on women in sport deserve special recognition.

Chapter 1

Timid Beginnings, 1900-1930

The 1890s have been described as years of transition in the lives of American women. Higher education was within their reach; their legal status was improving in many states; opportunities in the elite professions of medicine and law were increasing; and dress reform was beginning to free the female from the metal corset stays that often made even breathing difficult and from the petticoats, floor-length skirts, and long-sleeved shirtwaists that could collectively weigh as much as twenty pounds. Bicycling became a national craze, and basketball, invented for men, was immediately adopted by women as the team sport of the decade.

By the turn of the century the "new woman" often held a job prior to her marriage or she might even have chosen a career over marriage. The Gibson Girl, Charles Dana Gibson's artistic typification of the new woman, was frequently depicted playing tennis or golf, riding a bicycle, or driving an automobile. Sport was no longer an exclusively masculine realm.

Yet compared with today, women's opportunities to participate in sport around the turn of the century seem meager and society's willingness to accept such involvement limited. Women made a timid entry into the 1900 Paris Olympics in exhibition tennis and golf, while they saw the women's marathon accepted as an Olympic event in 1984. Materials written about women's sports throughout the twentieth century put this early period into perspective and further document the progress and changes that have since occurred. Although information published between 1900 and 1930 is sparse, it nonetheless paints a sweeping picture of the landscape of women in sport at that time.

1900

1   SMART, ISABELLE THOMPSON. *The Question of Heavy Apparatus Work for Women*. Boston: American Gymnasia Co., n.d., 14 pp.

Presents the medical view of a female physician about the use of heavy apparatus in gymnastics work for woman. Advises caution in exercising because of lack of physiological knowledge about women.

1901

1   BERENSON, SENDA, ed. *Line Basket Ball for Women*. New York: American Sports Publishing Co., 62 pp.

Contains the first published rules for women's basketball. An editorial provides background information for the development of the rules, and articles on the psychological and physiological effects of basketball on women provide insight into the game at the turn of the century. Official rules for playing the game are detailed, as well as the editor's prevailing philosophy about the sport.

2   PARET, J. PARMLY. *The Woman's Book of Sport*. New York: D. Appleton & Co., 172 pp.

Written as an instructional manual on sports for women; includes information on golf, tennis, sailing a catboat, swimming, bicycling, and basketball. Offers advice on exercises for healthful physical development and provides information about men's sports so women can be intelligent spectators at such events. Captures the turn-of-the-century flavor of women's sports in the photographs of women participants.

1902

1   HECKER, GENEVIEVE. *Golf for Women*. New York: Harper & Brothers, 217 pp.

Analyzes the skills of the game of golf; offers suggestions for playing the long game and the short game. By contemporary standards, the book will appear quaint, but it provides a good picture of the status of golf for women at the turn of the century.

1903

1 HILL, LUCILLE EATON. *Athletic and Outdoor Sports for Women.* New York: Macmillan Co., 339 pp.

One of the earliest publications in the United States devoted exclusively to women's sports. Describes a variety of 1903 activities for women including basketball, hockey, golf, tennis, rowing, track athletics, horseback riding, and cross-country walking. The introduction provides an enlightened view of the value of sports for women in the early 1900s. Illustrations for each of the activities provide a pictorial history of women's sports for this period.

1906

1 BEARD, LINA, and BEARD, ADELIA. *Recreations for Girls.* New York: Charles Scribner's Sons, 369 pp.

Describes numerous activities by which a young girl may amuse herself. Most are sedentary, indoor activities with only a few physical activities mentioned.

1908

1 CLAPP, ANNE BARR, and POUND, LOUISE, eds. *Collegiate Basket Ball Rules for Women.* Lincoln, Neb.: The University Publishing Co., 32 pp.

Outlines rules for a five-player, full-court game based on rules used by college men. Unusual for a time when virtually all college women played the game on a three-division court with six or more players. Includes information on the need for direction in women's athletics in general and the value of basketball as a socializing agent for women.

1909

1 DUDLEY, GERTRUDE, and KELLOR, FRANCES A. *Athletic Games in the Education of Women*. New York: Henry Holt & Co., 274 pp.

Clarifies the educational values of team sports for women and provides a general feeling for the prevailing philosophy about such activities for women. In addition to values of athletic games, the authors also describe the present conditions of competitive games in high schools, colleges, and organizations. A concluding section provides instructional techniques and general suggestions for teaching basketball, indoor baseball, and field hockey to women.

1914

1 BOLTON, FLORENCE. *Exercises for Women*. New York: Funk & Wagnalls Co., 141 pp.

Primarily concerned with calisthenics for women, but also contains information that is related to attitudes about physical activity for women at the time. In a chapter entitled "Clothes an Important Factor," the author discusses in great detail the kind of clothes appropriate for activity, covering everything from corset to shoes. Such topics as the bath in relation to exercise and the proper time of day for exercise are presented; concluding chapters describe and illustrate a series of exercises.

1916

1 BJURSTEDT, MOLLA. *Tennis for Women*. New York: Doubleday Page & Co., 181 pp.

Written by one of the top women competitors in the early 1900s and one of the few instructional texts directed toward women's play. Discusses the skills and strategy for playing the game; provides a historical view of tennis as played by women in this time period.

2 HASKINS, MABEL S. *Golf for Women (by a Woman Golfer)*. New York: Moffat, Yard & Co., 275 pp.

Offers detailed instructions for learning and playing the game of golf. Urges the development of understanding mechanical principles and applying them to all phases of the game. Discusses the causes of bad form and ways of correcting them. Numerous photographs of women golfers of the time should be of historical interest.

1920

1   BOCKER, DOROTHY. *Basket Ball for Women.* New York: Thomas E. Wilson & Co., 109 pp.

Analyzes basic skills necessary to play the game of basketball; offers suggestions for team play. Outlines the duties of officials and suggests planned plays for game use. Includes information on safety, basketball for working girls or for those who wish to coach, and basketball in the training of teachers. Well illustrated with photographs.

2   FROST, HELEN, and WARDLAW, CHARLES DIGBY. *Basket Ball and Indoor Baseball for Women.* New York: Charles Scribner's Sons, 171 pp.

Presents detailed instructions and skill analysis for playing the games of basketball (the three-division court game) and indoor baseball. Includes team strategies; is generously illustrated with photographs. An introduction to the book by Thomas E. Wood discusses the values of team sports for girls and women.

3   LENGLEN, SUZANNE. *Lawn Tennis for Girls.* New York: American Sports Publishing Co., 104 pp.

Analyzes skills and tactics of the game of tennis; offers corrections for common faults and miscellaneous hints for improving game play. Today's players may smile at the chapter on "Tennis Clothes for Women," but may still find some of the advice recommended by the first woman professional player quite useful.

1921

1   MENZIES, MRS. STUART. *The Woman's Book of Sports.* London: Vinton & Co., 317 pp.

Written as an instructional manual for the potential sportswoman with a major focus on hunting and fishing (twenty-four chapters). Remaining chapters provide information on fencing, golf, tennis, skiing, swimming, and flying.

1923

1   FROST, HELEN, and CUBBERLEY, HAZEL J. *Field Hockey and Soccer for Women*. New York: Charles Scribner's Sons, 264 pp.

Analyzes playing skills for soccer and hockey. Offers suggestions for practice, both indoors and outdoors, and suggestions for coaching the games.

2   HANDLEY, LOUIS de B. *Swimming for Women*. New York: American Sports Publishing Co., 151 pp.

Analyzes basic swimming and diving skills; encourages competitive swimming for women and offers training suggestions. Includes lifesaving techniques and ideas for practicing swimming techniques at home.

1926

1   COTTERAL, BONNIE, and COTTERAL, DONNIE. *Tumbling, Pyramid Building, and Stunts for Girls and Women*. New York: A.S. Barnes & Co., 143 pp.

Analyzes skills for a variety of stunts and tumbling activities, including combinations of skills for building pyramids. Offers teaching suggestions and ideas for presenting demonstration programs.

2   STABELL, HALLDIS. *Renaissance of the Body Through Scientific-Aesthetic Physical Education*. San Francisco: Harr Wagner Publishing Co., 72 pp.

Clarifies the need for a special approach to women's exercise. Analyzes exercises for bodily improvement; discusses the relationship between such routine actions as sitting down to health and beauty.

1927

1   COOPER, COURTNEY RYLEY. *Annie Oakley, Woman at Arms*. New York: Duffield & Co., 271 pp.

Describes the life and career of Annie Oakley, successful markswoman of the nineteenth century and star in the traveling Wild West shows of the time.

2   JOHNSON, GEORGIA BORG. *Organization of the Required Physical Education Program for Women in State Universities.* New York: Teachers College, Columbia University, 179 pp.

Describes the required physical education programs for women in fifteen selected universities. Clarifies the nature of activities, evaluation procedures, class policy, and standards for faculty. Includes a brief section on intercollegiate athletics for women.

3   SUMPTION, DOROTHY. *Fundamental Danish Gymnastics for Women.* New York: A.S. Barnes & Co., 219 pp.

Designed "for use of only those who are trained in the teaching of gymnastics" (p. ix). Focuses on techniques for teaching Danish gymnastics; includes organizational procedures, lesson plans, and skill analysis for gymnastic exercises.

1928

1   COLLETT, GLENNA. *Ladies in the Rough.* New York: Alfred A. Knopf, 237 pp.

Chronicles the golfing career of one of the early, successful women on the golf circuit, Glenna Collett. Includes a number of references to and brief comments about prominent women players of the era. Concludes with instructions for beginning players and suggestions for developing the "tournament mind."

2   CUBBERLEY, HELEN J. *Field Hockey Analyzed for Instructor and Player.* New York: A.S. Barnes & Co., 203 pp.

Presents an approach for teaching field hockey techniques. Discusses basic principles such as angles and leverage so important to hockey; suggests teaching methods for beginning players.

3   EARHART, AMELIA. *20 Hrs. 40 Min.* New York: G.P. Putnam's Sons, 314 pp. Reprint. New York: Arno Press, 1980.

Presents Earhart's autobiography including her early interest in airplanes, acquiring her first plane, and her experience as the first woman passenger on a transatlantic flight. Discusses women in aviation, the problems they faced, and the progress made by women in the field of flying.

4 FRYMIR, ALICE W. *Basket Ball for Women*. New York: A.S. Barnes & Co., 285 pp.

Designed as a complete book on basketball for teacher, coach, and player. Includes history of the game, responsibility of the coach for physical and social ideals, individual and team techniques for game play, and instructions for officials. Health of the player is discussed, and a final chapter focuses on appropriate competitive activities. Throughout, the book reflects the standards and policies of women's athletics as espoused by most women in physical education in the 1920s.

5 JOHNSTON, CHARLES H. L. *Famous American Athletes of Today*. Boston: L.C. Page & Co., 15 volumes (editors after volume 5 vary).

Presents a collection of biographical sketches of top American athletes between the years 1928 and 1958, many of whom are women. A list of athletes and location of source follows: Tenley Albright, vol. 14, 1956, pp. 1-14; Patty Berg, .vol. 7, 1940, pp. 305-340; Evelyn Chandler, vol. 8, 1942, pp. 63-84; Glenna Collett, vol. 2, 1930, pp. 91-114; Maureen Connolly, vol. 13, 1953, pp. 23-42; Sarah Palfrey Cooke, vol. 8, 1942, pp. 153-176; Mildred "Babe" Didrikson, vol. 3, 1932, pp. 65-84; Amelia Earhart, vol. 2, 1930, pp. 115-138; Gertrude Ederle, vol. 1, 1928, pp. 275-310; Helen Hicks, vol. 3, 1932, pp. 107-124; Eleanor Holm, vol. 4, 1934, pp. 73-88; Helen Hull Jacobs, vol. 4, 1934, pp. 101-126; Helene Madison, vol. 4, 1934, pp. 73-88; Alice Marble, vol. 7, 1940, pp. 305-340; Gertrude "Gussie" Moran, vol. 12, 1951, pp. 275-296; Katherine Rawls, vol. 6, 1938, pp. 199-230; Helen Stephens, vol. 5, 1937, pp. 339-370; Virginia Van Wie, vol. 4, 1934, pp. 207-216; Hazel Hotchkiss Wightman, vol. 5, 1937, pp. 371-398; Helen Wills, vol. 1, 1928, pp. 211-234.

6 MONTGOMERY, KATHERINE W. *Volleyball for Women*. New York: A.S. Barnes & Co., 104 pp.

Presents an unusual approach to volleyball play with seven persons on a team and three hits to a side when women generally played with eight players and six hits. Analyzes game skills and strategy; suggests practice drills. Includes a summary of rules described as the Florida State Volleyball Rules for Women.

7 SMITH, HELEN N., and COOPS, HELEN LESLIE. *Play Days*. New York: A.S. Barnes & Co., 45 pp.

Defines the purpose of the play day for girls and women; suggests activities and organizational procedures for conducting a play day.

1929

1   ANDERSON, LOU EASTWOOD. *Basketball for Women.* New York: The Macmillan Co., 143 pp.

Designed as a text primarily for teachers, but usable by players also. Analyzes the skills of the game and suggests self-testing techniques for evaluating skills. Photographs and the narrative provide an overview of the nature of basketball for women in 1929.

2   DUNCAN, MARGARET H., and CUNDIFF, VELDA P. *Play Days for Girls and Women.* New York: A.S. Barnes & Co., 87 pp.

Focuses on the play day developed in the 1920s as a "type of athletic competition . . . which is socially sound as well as physically wholesome" (p. v). Describes in detail the nature of the play day which was offered as a substitute for the more highly competitive programs under scrutiny at the time. Emphasis is placed on participation by everyone, and the authors outline all the information necessary for planning and conducting a play day from that philosophical viewpoint.

3   HILLAS, MARJORIE, and KNIGHTON, MARIAN. *Athletic Programs for High School and College Women.* New York: A.S. Barnes & Co., 102 pp.

Concerns the development and organization of a progressive program of women's athletics for high schools and colleges. Focuses on the team sports of soccer, field hockey, basketball, baseball, and speedball with skill analysis and teaching suggestions for each sport. Includes informational materials for conducting a play day, the generally accepted form of competition for women.

4   PALMER, GLADYS E. *Baseball for Girls and Women.* New York: A.S. Barnes & Co., 150 pp.

Provides analysis of the skills and techniques for playing baseball; includes rules for both the indoor and outdoor games. Designed primarily as a teaching guide for the sports.

5   PERRIN, ETHEL, and TURNER, GRACE. *Play Day: The Spirit of Sport*. New York: American Child Health Association, 77 pp.
    Discusses values and conduct of play days, a substitute for varsity-type athletics for girls.

1930

1   AINSWORTH, DOROTHY S. *The History of Physical Education in Colleges for Women*. New York: A.S. Barnes & Co., 131 pp.
    Outlines the development of physical education for college women from a study of twelve women's colleges. Includes information about curriculum, facilities and equipment, staff, organizational procedures, and competitive programs for women. Offers a good overview of the nature of physical education activities for women in 1930.

2   BURR, HILDA V. *Field Hockey for Coaches and Players*. New York: A.S. Barnes & Co., 208 pp.
    Focuses on the skills and tactics for playing field hockey. Includes skill analysis, offensive and defensive strategy, practice drills, and hints for coaches and umpires.

3   FRYMIR, ALICE W. *Track and Field for Women*. New York: A.S. Barnes & Co., 224 pp.
    Deals primarily with the techniques for learning track and field skills. Includes a brief history of track and field and suggestions for training and conditioning. More than fifty photographs provide an historical overview of techniques in use at the time.

4   NATIONAL AMATEUR ATHLETIC FEDERATION, WOMEN'S DIVISION, eds. *Women and Athletics*. New York: A. S. Barnes & Co., 95 pp.
    Contains a collection of nineteen papers dealing with diverse topics related to women's athletics. Such provocative titles as "Safeguarding Girls' Athletics," "Are State Championships Educationally Sound?" and "The Playtime of a Million Girls or an Olympic Victory–Which?" are suggestive of prevailing attitudes toward athletics for women. Describes the activities, aims, and platform of beliefs of the Women's Division, National Amateur Athletic Federation

which was founded in 1923 and exerted considerable influence on women's sports for almost twenty years.

5   POLLARD, MARJORIE. *Learning to Play Field Hockey.* New York: American Sports Publishing Co., 74 pp.

Focuses on the fundamental skills of field hockey for beginning players. Includes skill analysis and offensive and defensive tactics.

6   SOMERS, FLORENCE A. *Principles of Women's Athletics.* New York: A.S. Barnes & Co., 151 pp.

Provides basic principles for the selection and conduct of athletic programs for girls and women. Discusses factors related to women's participation, current trends in participation and competition, and conditions that have influenced the development of sports for women. Includes a list of principles for the development of women's programs with supporting and clarifying commentary for each statement. A general feeling that the author is dealing with a "problem," women's athletics, pervades the book; however, she provides insight into the attitudes toward women's involvement in sport that prevailed at the time.

Chapter 2

Play Days and Olympic Medals, 1931-1960

The decade of the 1930s began with the nation under the black cloud of the Great Depression. Working women faced severe difficulties in the job market, and professional women had their wages and hours cut and found little opportunity for advancement in their chosen fields. With the onset of World War II in 1941 remarkable changes occurred in the lives of many women. The military uniform, traditional symbol of masculinity, was worn for the first time by women with the founding of the Women's Army Corps, the Navy Waves, the Women Marines, and the Coast Guard SPARS. Rosie the Riveter came to symbolize the woman in the workforce during wartime. Following the war, in the late 1940s and 1950s, the number of working women continued to rise, but the importance of marriage and motherhood as the goal of women was again emphasized.

For the American sportswoman, as for women in general, the years between 1930 and 1960 were paradoxical. A number of athletes had emerged in the Golden Age of Sport, the 1920s. Though perhaps not household names, Glenna Collett, Helen Wills, Gertrude Ederle, Eleonora Sears, Aileen Riggen, Amelia Earhart, and Eleanor Holmes were surely well known to the American public when Wall Street collapsed. Soon after, Babe Didrikson began to make headlines, capturing the nation's interest in 1932 with outstanding performances in track and field and her one silver and two gold medals in the 1932 Olympic Games.

In opposition to the promotion of highly competitive activities for women were the Women's Division of the National Amateur Athletic Federation, established in 1923, and the National Section on Women's Athletics, a professional organization of women physical educators. Both groups espoused a philosophy encompassed in the motto, "A sport for every girl, a girl in every sport." Participation, not competition, was the goal. In high schools and colleges throughout the country play days and sports days, both of which deemphasized the competitive aspect of sport, were replacing varsity athletics. With few exceptions, the highly skilled high school or college female athlete had little opportunity to pursue excellence.

Outside of school, however, the picture was different. The Amateur Athletic Union regularly sponsored competitive events in a number of sports, and amateur golf and tennis flourished with national and international competition available in both sports. The All American Girls' Professional Baseball League was established in 1943 and operated until 1954, offering unique opportunities in professional sport to women. The Redheads, a professional women's basketball team, began touring with exhibition games in 1948. Until the 1960s, however, sports opportunities for women were still quite limited when compared with those for men. Great women athletes can nonetheless be identified in the decades between 1930 and 1960, and some opportunities were available to them in both amateur and professional sport. Perhaps it was Wilma Rudolph's three gold medals in the 1960 Rome Olympics that heralded the winds of change in the succeeding decades.

1932

1   EARHART, AMELIA. *The Fun of It*. New York: Harcourt, Brace & Co., 1932, 218 pp. Reprint. Detroit: Gale Research Co., 1975.
    Describes Earhart's early involvement with flying and her experiences as a flyer. Profiles some of the early women pioneers in flying such as Ruth Nichols, Elinor Smith, and Katherine Stinson.

1933

1   POST, JULIA H., and SHIRLEY, MABEL J. *Selected Recreational Sports for Girls and Women*. New York: A.S. Barnes & Co., 151 pp.
    Identifies several activities that may be enjoyed as recreation and offers a rationale for including these in an instructional school program. Skills, rules, and strategy are included for deck tennis, horseshoe pitching, table tennis, shuffleboard, clock golf, paddle tennis, and tetherball.

1934

1   WAYMAN, AGNES R. *Education Through Physical Education*. Philadelphia: Lea & Febiger, 393 pp.

Presents one of the earliest women's points of view concerning the organization and administration of physical education programs for girls and women. Includes administrative procedures for all program phases. An emphasis on sports programs for all girls and women, not merely the highly skilled, under the leadership of women pervades the book.

1935

1   FRYMIR, ALICE W., and HILLAS, MARJORIE. *Team Sports for Women*. New York: A.S. Barnes & Co., 215 pp.

Focuses on skills and strategies for learning the team sports, baseball, basketball, hockey, soccer, speedball, and volleyball. Includes a section on officiating techniques for those sports as well as a brief section on methods of teaching.

1936

1   FORD, MARY ELIZABETH. *Little Women Grow Bold*. Boston: Bruce Humphrie, 242 pp.

Contains biographical information for a selection of sportswomen "who have already achieved their prime" (p. 7). Includes swimmers Annette Kellerman, Gertrude Ederle; tennis players May Sutton, Hazel Hotchkiss, Mary K. Browne, Molla (Mallory) Bjurstedt, Suzanne Lenglen, Helen Wills; golfers Elaine Rosenthal, Margaret Curtis, Dorothy Campbell, Glenna Collett, Joyce Wethered; flyers Amelia Earhart, Katherine Stinson, Phoebe Omlie; runners Babe Didrikson, Stella Walsh; and sharpshooter Annie Oakley. Very brief notes are included for women in a variety of other activities: billiards, bullfighting, archery, fencing, fishing, rodeo, sailing, and figure skating and such daredevil activities as lion taming, acrobatics, and riding over Niagara Falls in a barrel.

2   JACOBS, HELEN HULL. *Beyond the Game, An Autobiography*. Philadelphia: J.B. Lippincott Co., 276 pp.

Details the life and amateur tennis career of the author. Written, as Jacobs notes in the preface, because it should be done by "someone who was in possession of the facts" (p. 7).

3 TOWNSEND, ANNE B. *Field Hockey.* New York: Charles Scribner's Sons, 161 pp.

Though not identified as field hockey for women only, uses the feminine gender throughout the book. Covers individual skills, position play and tactics and strategy for team play. Concludes with a narrative on competition and the amateur status of hockey.

1937

1 LEE, MABEL. *The Conduct of Physical Education.* New York: A.S. Barnes & Co., 584 pp.

Designed as a textbook for professional physical educators. Details administrative procedures for conducting a program for girls and women; identifies necessary equipment and facilities; reviews activities for curricular offerings; and discusses budget, evaluation, and scheduling. A discussion of competition clarifies the prevailing philosophic view among many women physical educators regarding interschool competition for girls and women.

1938

1 WAYMAN, AGNES R. *A Modern Philosophy of Physical Education.* Philadelphia: W.B. Saunders Co., 231 pp.

Details the principles and philosophy underlying the conduct of physical education programs for girls and women. Provides a general overview of the nature of physical education programs as they existed in the 1930s under the leadership of women.

1940

1 HENIE, SONJA. *Wings on My Feet.* New York: Prentice-Hall, 184 pp.

Presents an autobiographical sketch of Henie's life as an amateur and professional skater. Devotes about half of the book to instructions for learning the intricacies of figure skating and how to improve one's skill in the sport.

2   MEISSNER, WILHELMINE E., and MEYERS, ELIZABETH YEEND. *Basketball for Girls*. New York: A.S. Barnes & Co., 84 pp.
    Written for "persons who have a general basic understanding of the game" (p. v). Includes a brief history of the game, skill analysis, offensive and defensive strategies, and officiating techniques. Skills are illustrated with drawings; numerous diagrams for drills are included.

3   SUMPTION, DOROTHY. *Sports for Women*. New York: Prentice-Hall, 275 pp.
    Focuses on the organization and administration of college women's recreational activities including club sports, intramural and intercollegiate competition, and corecreational activities. Of particular interest are the descriptions of play days, sports days, and dual meets identified as intercollegiate competition in relation to the contemporary view and definition of intercollegiate athletics.

1941

1   KENNARD, ADA B. *Tips on Girl's Basketball*. Detroit: Sport Tips & Teaching Aids, 31 pp.
    Organized in workbook form; contains diagrams and explanations of basic game skills, fouls, offensive and defensive strategy, duties of officials, and practice drills.

2   SEFTON, ALICE ALLENE. *The Women's Division, National Amateur Athletic Federation: Sixteen Years of Progress in Athletics for Girls and Women, 1923-1939*. Stanford, Calif.: Stanford University Press, 88 pp.
    Describes the general philosophy and historical development of the Women's Division and its promotion of wholesome sports for girls. Details the aims of the Division in twelve essays written by women who were leaders in the organization. Devotes one section to the kinds of work the group performed such as conferences, research, field work, and publications. Provides an excellent view of sports for women which was supported by many individuals and organizations in the 1920s and 1930s.

1942

1   ADAMS, JEAN, and KIMBALL, MARGARET. *Heroines of the Sky*. New York: Doubleday, 319 pp.

Presents biographical sketches for seventeen women who pioneered as flyers. Ranges from Harriet Quimby, the first American woman licensed as a pilot in 1911 to Gladys O'Donnell, a prominent competitive racing flyer of the 1930s.

2   BROCKETT, MARY LAIRD. *Tips on Field Hockey*. Detroit: Sport Tips & Teaching Aids, 69 pp.

Outlines the history of field hockey; analyzes game skills; presents helpful hints for the hockey teacher and suggestions for the beginning learner.

3   LEES, JOSEPHINE T. *Field Hockey for Girls*. New York: A.S. Barnes & Co., 88 pp.

Outlines the history of field hockey and equipment needed for play. Analyzes skills of the game and offensive and defensive tactics. Discusses umpiring techniques.

4   MEYER, MARGARET H., and SCHWARZ, MARGUERITE M. *Technic of Team Sports for Women*. Philadelphia: W.B. Saunders Co., 392 pp.

Offers a comprehensive treatment of techniques for teaching the team sports, basketball, field hockey, soccer, softball, speedball, and volleyball. Teaching methods and suggested drill formations provide a general introduction; history, individual skills and tactics, team strategy, position play, and care of equipment are included for each sport.

1943

1   AINSWORTH, DOROTHY S., et al. *Individual Sports for Women*. Philadelphia: W.B. Saunders Co., 397 pp.

Develops a rationale for the inclusion of individual and dual sports in programs for girls and women. Includes instructional techniques and game strategies where appropriate for archery, badminton, fencing, golf, riding, swimming, tennis, and bowling. A

18

section on tournaments identifies several different approaches to competition in the activities.

2   MARBLE, ALICE. *The Road to Wimbledon*. New York: Charles Scribner's Sons, 167 pp.
      Describes in detail Marble's early life, her introduction to tennis, and her experiences along the way to her successful win at Wimbledon in 1939.

3   MITCHELL, VIOLA. *Softball for Girls*. New York: A.S. Barnes & Co., 128 pp.
      Gives a brief history of baseball and its introduction to girls. Analyzes techniques of the game; offers suggestions for coaching and officiating.

1947

1   YOCOM, RACHAEL B., and HUNSAKER, H. B. *Individual Sports for Men and Women*. New York: A.S. Barnes & Co., 296 pp.
      One of the earliest texts focusing on teaching sports in a coeducational setting. Introduces a philosophy and rationale for the coed approach and includes instructional techniques for several activities appropriate to that approach such as archery, badminton, tennis, fencing, and golf.

1949

1   HENDERSON, EDWIN BANCROFT. "Negro Girls in Sport." In *The Negro in Sport*. Washington, D.C.: The Associated Publishers, pp. 230-242.
      Identifies athletic accomplishments of a number of black female athletes. Highlights competitors in golf, swimming, tennis, basketball, and track and field.

2   JACOBS, HELEN HULL. *Gallery of Champions*. Freeport, N.Y.: Books for Libraries Press, 232 pp.
      Focuses on the tennis careers of fifteen players who were champions in their respective countries, against whom the author

competed. Includes a number of personal anecdotes; offers unusual insight into the action on the court during matches with the following opponents: Suzanne Lenglen, Helen Wills Roark, Hilde Krahvinkel Sperling, Alice Marble, Dorothy Round Little, Molla Mallory Bjurstedt, Pauline Betz, Simone Mathieu, Cilli Aussem, Sarah Palfrey Cooke, Anita Lizana Ellis, Louise Brough, Margaret Osborne du Pont, Betty Nuthall, and Margaret Scriven Vivien.

1950

1 GARST, DORIS SHANNON. *Amelia Earhart: Heroine of the Skies*. New York: Julian Messner, 199 pp.

   Describes Earhart's life and career in the field of aviation, including her last flight from which she did not return.

1952

1 STUMP, AL J. *Champions Against Odds*. Philadelphia: Macrae Smith Co., 255 pp.

   Details the struggles faced by women athletes to achieve success in the 1940s when sports opportunities were limited for them. Includes divers Vicki Draves (pp. 33-43) and Pat McCormick (pp. 149-163); swimmer Nancy Merki (pp. 75-82); and skier Gretchen Fraser (pp. 214-220).

1953

1 MARSLAND, ANITRA M. *I Married a Boat*. New York: Abelard Press, 256 pp.

   Describes the author's experiences with a husband who was a sailing enthusiast and the importance of the boat to their long and successful marriage.

2 SPAIN, NANCY. *"Teach" Tennant*. London: Werner Laurie, 112 pp.

   Details the life and career of Eleanor "Teach" Tennant, ranked third as a tennis player in the United States in 1919, but better known, perhaps, as the coach for champions such as Maureen Connolly, Alice Marble, and Pauline Betz. Discusses at length Tennant's coaching techniques and hints for the making of a champion.

3   SUGGS, LOUISE. *Par Golf for Women*. New York: Prentice-Hall, 128 pp.

Offers complete instructions to the would-be golfer ranging from etiquette on the course and technical analysis of strokes, to common faults in golf and corrections for them. Skills are illustrated with photographs.

1954

1   CAMP, HERBERT PRESTON. *Coaching High School Girls' Basket Ball*. Douglasville, Ga.: County Sentinel, 50 pp.

Describes techniques and strategies used by Camp in coaching competitive high school girls' basketball. Diagrams specific plays for various game situations.

2   DAVIS, MAC. *100 Greatest Sports Heroes*. New York: Grosset & Dunlap, 156 pp.

Briefly describes the sports careers of Florence Chadwick (p. 15), Maureen Connolly (p. 21), Babe Didrikson (pp. 30-31), Gertrude Ederle (p. 36), Sonja Henie (p. 52), Suzanne Lenglen (p. 68), Annie Oakley (pp. 87-88), Stella Walsh (p. 134), and Helen Wills (pp. 140-141).

3   LAWRENCE, HELEN B., and FOX, GRACE I. *Basketball for Girls and Women*. New York: McGraw-Hill Book Co., 267 pp.

Offers comprehensive coverage of broad aspects of the game of basketball. Includes a section on sportsmanship for players, coaches, and spectators followed by a lengthy discussion of competition. Covers analysis of individual skills, offensive and defensive strategies, and care and prevention of injuries. Discusses officiating techniques; concludes with a history of the game and a chronology of the rules.

1955

1   DAY, BETH. *America's First Cowgirl: Lucille Mulhall*. New York: Julian Messner, 192 pp.

Details the life and accomplishments of Lucille Mulhall, one of the few women who competed against men in the early years of organized rodeo. Describes her success in steer roping and racing.

2 HART, DORIS. *Tennis with Hart*. Philadelphia: J.B. Lippincott Co., 192 pp.

Focuses primarily on Hart's tennis career with an introductory chapter about her childhood life and a serious knee operation at the age of fifteen months. Reports on many of her world travels related to tennis; an interesting chapter on Wimbledon where she won the singles title in 1951 discusses the insider's view of the Wimbledon tournament.

3 LeLEEUW, ADELE LOUISE. *Story of Amelia Earhart*. New York: Grosset & Dunlap, 181 pp.

Presents biographical information about Amelia Earhart; focuses on her personal life, her interest in flying, and her experiences as a flyer.

4 MILLER, DONNA MAE, and LEY, KATHERINE L. *Individual and Team Sports for Women*. New York: Prentice-Hall, 511 pp.

Designed as an instruction manual for teachers. Includes materials and methods common to all sports such as use of audiovisual aids; ways of teaching skills, strategies, and rules simultaneously; drill formations; and effective tournaments. For each sport, archery, badminton, bowling, golf, skating, skiing, tennis, track and field, basketball, field hockey, speedball, softball, and volleyball, the following information appears: history, skill analysis, strategies, evaluation techniques, teaching aids, and suggestions for class organization and progression.

5 ZAHARIAS, BABE DIDRIKSON. *This Life I've Led*. New York: A. S. Barnes & Co., 255 pp.

Meets the expectations one might have from the title. Chronicles Zaharias's athletic career and her experiences in a variety of different sports. At least half of the book focuses on her golfing career. Later sections discuss her responses to the diagnosis of cancer, which, ultimately, was the cause of her death.

1956

1 FITZGERALD, EDWARD E. "Little Mo–Queen at Sixteen." In *Champions in Sports and Spirit*. New York: Farrar, Straus & Cudahy, pp. 57-84.

Provides biographical information about Maureen "Little Mo" Connolly and her tennis career up to the time of her marriage in 1955 when she retired from tennis after breaking a leg in a riding accident.

1958

1 DUSHEATH, JOYCE; REID, HILDA; GREGORY, EILEEN; and DELANY, FRANCES. *Mountains and Memsahibs*. London: Constable & Co., 208 pp.

Details the trip made by the four authors up the Bora Shigri Glacier in the Himalayas, including the automobile trip from London to Manali, India, their departure point for the climb. Includes descriptive accounts of both the overland trip and the mountain climbing experience.

2 GARST, SHANNON. *Annie Oakley*. New York: Julian Messner, 190 pp.

Describes Oakley's childhood years, her career in the circus and wild west shows, and her retirement from show business after being injured in a serious train accident.

3 GIBSON, ALTHEA. *I Always Wanted to Be Somebody*. New York: Harper & Brothers, 186 pp.

Describes Gibson's early life and growing up in New York where the family moved from her birthplace in South Carolina. Discusses her introduction to tennis by way of paddle tennis played in the streets, her collegiate career, and her successful win at Wimbledon. Offers unusual insights into her life in the predominantly white world of tennis.

4 MULL, EVELYN. *Women in Sports Car Competition*. New York: Sports Car Press, 105 pp.

Identifies a number of women automobile racing competitors and why they began a sport usually reserved for men. Includes a brief history of early twentieth century racing, clarifies different kinds of auto races, and offers suggestions on what to race and where.

5   PATERSON, ANN, ed. *Team Sports for Girls*. New York: Ronald Press Co., 403 pp.

   Designed as a textbook for teachers of team sports. Includes skill analysis, rules summary, and offensive and defensive strategy for basketball, field hockey, lacrosse, soccer, speedball, speed-a-way, softball, and volleyball.

6   REDIN, HARLEY J. *The Queens Fly High*. Plainview, Tex.: Harley J. Redin, 186 pp.

   Analyzes individual skills and team strategy for basketball; offers a variety of practice drills, suggestions for scouting, organizing tournament play, and care and prevention of injuries. Written by the coach of the successful Wayland Baptist College team, the Flying Queens, the book contains a number of photos of team players as well as a brief history of the team.

1960

1   BRIAND, PAUL, Jr. *Daughter of the Sky: The Story of Amelia Earhart*. New York: Duell, Sloan & Pearce, 247 pp.

   Chronicles Earhart's life and her avid enthusiasm for flying. Reports one version of the end of her career in which she and Fred Noonan were captured by the Japanese as spies after a forced landing in the Pacific.

2   SEIBERT, JERRY. *Amelia Earhart: First Lady of the Air*. Boston: Houghton Mifflin Co., 191 pp.

   Presents biographical information about Earhart in the form of a story for young readers. Includes her early life and her experiences as a flyer.

3   SUGGS, LOUISE, ed. *Golf for Women*. New York: Doubleday & Co., 192 pp.

   Offers a detailed analysis of golf skills with each section written by a famous woman player. All techniques are illustrated; tips for success follow the instructions for each golf shot. Concludes with etiquette for the course and rules of the game.

4   VANNIER, MARYHELEN, and POINDEXTER, HALLY BETH.
    Individual and Team Sports for Girls and Women. Philadelphia: W.B.
    Saunders Co., 591 pp.
        Written as an instruction manual for teachers and learners
    with an introduction clarifying the unique contributions of sport
    participation. Nature of the game, equipment and facilities, skill
    analysis, game strategy, officiating techniques, teaching aids, and lead-
    up games are described for each of the following activities: archery,
    badminton, bowling, fencing, golf, swimming, diving, synchronized
    swimming, table tennis, tennis, track and field, basketball, field hockey,
    lacrosse, soccer, softball, speedball, and volleyball.

Chapter 3

The Winds of Change, 1961-1975

The sixties and seventies were decades of change for women. They were entering the workforce in increasing numbers; sex discrimination in the workplace was prohibited by Title VII of the Civil Rights Act; and the Equal Pay Act mandated equal pay for equal work. Women had gained more control over their lives through new birth-control technology, and the feminist movement emerged. With the passage of Title IX of the Educational Amendments Act in 1972, sex discrimination was prohibited in any educational program receiving federal funds. Women's studies courses were introduced in colleges around the country, and women banded together in their own organizations, the National Organization for Women (NOW), the Women's Equity Action League (WEAL), and the Women's Political Caucus.

For the aspiring sportswoman, opportunities for participation at all levels began to improve. Salaries for women in professional sports were increasing, though slowly, and women tennis players initiated their own professional tour following the formation of the Women's Tennis Association in 1970. Women were entering areas that had traditionally belonged to men. Roberta Gibb Bengay in 1966 and Kathy Switzer in 1967 managed to break the barriers of the Boston Marathon, albeit through subterfuge; Kathy Kusner became the first woman licensed to ride in thoroughbred races in 1968; and Diane Crump raced in the Kentucky Derby in 1970. Women entered the Olympic Games in increasing numbers, and a new team sport, volleyball, was added to the Olympic program in 1964, the first time such an addition had been made for women and men in the same year.

One of the most visible changes in opportunities was the escalating establishment of interscholastic and intercollegiate athletic programs for women. Such programs were neither novel nor new. Iowa had conducted high school girls' basketball competition, including a state tournament, for decades; colleges in Florida offered athletic scholarships to women in tennis and swimming. Women in physical education were reexamining the prevailing philosophy concerning sport for the masses, and their leaders began to recommend that highly skilled women be given opportunities to compete beyond the intramural level. Thus, in 1969, the Commission on Intercollegiate Athletics for Women, later the Association of Intercollegiate Athletics for Women (AIAW), sponsored its first national collegiate championships in golf, gymnastics, and track and field, adding badminton, volleyball, and swimming in 1970. With the passage of Title IX in 1972, athletic programs for high school and college women developed almost overnight. By 1975 virtually every high school in the nation offered female students some competitive opportunities; membership in the AIAW, the counterpart of the National Collegiate Athletic Association (NCAA), was climbing toward 900 member schools; and college-bound female athletes were beginning to select schools on the basis of the athletic scholarships proffered.

The literature concerning women in sport at this time is indicative of the massive changes occurring at all levels. Biographies of successful women athletes, both professional and amateur, are abundant, as are instructional manuals for the interested learner or teacher. Research-based information on women in sport appeared more often, along with information on conditioning, training, and coaching specifically for women. The range of topics concerning women in sport suggests the increasing involvement of girls and women in all kinds of activities and at all levels from the novice to the Olympic competitor.

1961

1   HALSEY, ELIZABETH. *Women in Physical Education: Their Role in Work, Home, and History*. New York: G.P. Putnam's Sons, 260 pp.

Examines the role of women in the physical education profession. Though not exclusively devoted to *sport* for women, the author includes biographical data for several women who have had an impact on women's sport such as Senda Berenson (basketball) and Constance Applebee (field hockey).

2   MILLER, HELEN MARKLEY. *Striving to Be Champion: Babe Didrikson Zaharias*. Chicago: Kingston House, 191 pp.

Chronicles Zaharias's athletic successes beginning with the 1932 Olympic Games until her death in 1956. Discusses her alternating between professional and amateur status; concludes with the battle she waged against cancer.

3   PARKER, ROBERT. *Carol Heiss, Olympic Queen*. Garden City, N.Y.: Doubleday & Co., 128 pp.

Describes Heiss' figure skating career from receiving her first pair of skates at the age of three and a half to her Olympic medal in the 1960 Winter Olympics.

4   VERMER, JEAN C. *The Girl's Book of Physical Fitness*. New York: Association Press, 135 pp.

Focuses on the values of exercise and good health and ways to achieve the latter. Discusses adolescent growth and change, graceful recreational activities for girls such as figure skating and horseback riding, and the relationship of physical fitness to a girl's future.

5   WACHTEL, ERNA, and LOKEN, NEWTON C. *Girls' Gymnastics*. New York: Sterling Publishing Co., 128 pp.

Analyzes skills performed on the balance beam, even and uneven parallel bars, and in free exercise and vaulting. Illustrates each skill with a photograph.

6   WIND, HERBERT WARREN. "G A M Inc.: Gussie Moran." In *The Gilded Age of Sport*. New York: Simon & Schuster, pp. 354-359.

Written at the time Moran was embarking on a career in broadcasting after leaving tennis. Briefly comments on her tennis career, especially her introduction of the lace-edged pants worn under her tennis dress and its controversy among the staid spectators at Wimbledon.

7   _____. "Xceed Xpectations, Yell Yours, Zip Zip." In *The Gilded Age of Sport*. New York: Simon & Schuster, pp. 380-421.

Profiles the Queen Mother of American tennis, Hazel Wightman, including biographical information about her life and tennis career. Focuses on her work in the promotion of tennis for women and her experiences as a teacher and coach.

1962

1   MORTIMER, ANGELA. *My Waiting Game*. London: Frederick Muller, 196 pp.

Describes the life and tennis career of the 1961 Wimbledon singles champion, Angela Mortimer.

2   PARLIN, JOHN. *Amelia Earhart: Pioneer in the Sky*. Champaign, Ill.: Garrard Publishing Co., 80 pp.

Briefly describes Earhart's introduction to the world of flying and her success as an aviator.

3   PUGH, D.L., and WATTS, D.V. *Athletics for Women*. London: Stanley Paul, 134 pp.

Written for use by the athlete herself. Skills are thoroughly analyzed with specific instructions for performance. A suggested training/practice schedule is provided for each track and field event.

4   TEAGUE, BERTHA FRANK. *Basketball for Girls*. New York: Ronald Press Co., 189 pp.

Analyzes individual skills and techniques for playing basketball; discusses offensive and defensive team play. Concludes with suggestions for coaching competitive teams which coaches in 1990 would likely view as quaint and old fashioned.

1963

1   HUGHES, ERIC, ed. *Gymnastics for Girls: A Competitive Approach for Teacher and Coach*. New York: Ronald Press Co., 275 pp.

Focuses on the teaching of gymnastics as a competitive sport. Analyzes skills performed in women's competitive events; describes safety procedures and guidelines for organizing competition.

2   MACKEY, HELEN T. *Field Hockey, An International Team Sport.* Englewood Cliffs, N.J.: Prentice Hall, 174 pp.

Presents skill analysis and strategy for game play, suggestions for playing the various team positions, and practice drills. Generously illustrated with photographs and drawings.

1964

1   BABBITT, DIANE H., and HAAS, WERNER. *Gymnastic Apparatus Exercises for Girls.* New York: Ronald Press Co., 138 pp.

Designed as a text for teaching apparatus work at the beginning and intermediate levels. Consists primarily of skill analysis for the exercises performed on apparatus.

2   BELL, MARY M. *Women's Basketball.* Dubuque, Iowa: William C. Brown Co., 76 pp.

Presents a brief history of women's basketball. Analyzes defensive and offensive skills and strategies for the six-player game with corrections for common errors; offers suggestions for coaching competitive teams.

3   BONTEMPS, ARNA. "Althea Gibson." In *Famous Negro Athletes.* New York: Dodd, Mead & Co., pp. 130-148.

Offers brief biographical information about Gibson, including her early life in Harlem and her route to success as the first black woman tennis champion at Forest Hills and Wimbledon.

4   FORSLUND, ELLEN. *Bowling for Women.* New York: Ronald Press Co., 94 pp.

Presents skills of bowling in a progressive level with progression determined by average scores achieved. Offers suggestions for left-handed and senior bowlers.

5   HYMAN, DOROTHY. *Sprint to Fame.* London: Stanley Paul, 159 pp.

Chronicles the eleven-year running career of Olympian Dorothy Hyman. Discusses her controversial view of amateurism and what she sees as her future in athletics beyond her age of twenty-three.

6   JACOBS, HELEN HULL. *Famous American Women Athletes*. New York: Dodd, Mead & Co., 121 pp.

Offers biographical sketches of a dozen women who achieved success in various sports, many of them athletes known personally by the author. Includes Ann Curtis and Aileen Riggin, swimming; Gretchen Fraser, skiing; Shirley Garms, bowling; Carol Heiss and Theresa Weld, figure skating; Floretta McCutcheon, bowling; Wilma Rudolph, track; Alice Marble and Helen Wills, tennis; Margaret Varner, squash racquets; and Babe Didrikson Zaharias, track and golf.

7   MACKEY, HELEN T., and MACKEY, ANN M. *Women's Team Sports Officiating*. New York: Ronald Press Co., 131 pp.

Details the techniques for developing officiating skills in basketball, field hockey, lacrosse, softball, and volleyball. Includes information about pregame preparation, postgame responsibilities, and the general qualities necessary for becoming a successful official.

8   MILLER, KENNETH D. *Track and Field for Girls*. New York: Ronald Press Co., 125 pp.

Describes the historical development of track and field for women; analyzes performance techniques for each of the events in which women participate; includes suggestions for conditioning.

9   SCOTT, PHEBE M. and CRAFTS, VIRGINIA R. *Track and Field for Girls and Women*. New York: Appleton-Century-Crofts, 237 pp.

Written as a practical manual for teachers when few such books specifically for women's track and field were available. Presents a brief history of track and field and skill analysis and teaching techniques for each event. A lengthy appendix includes practical materials useful in planning and conducting track and field competition.

10   VANNIER, MARYHELEN, and POINDEXTER, HALLY B.W. *Physical Activities for College Women*. Philadelphia: W.B. Saunders, 527 pp.

Clarifies the values of physical activity for women. Includes information on sixteen individual sports; eight team sports; and social, folk, square, and modern dance. Discusses sports competition for women.

1965

1   DULLES, FOSTER RHEA. *A History of Recreation: America Learns to Play*. New York: Appleton-Century-Crofts, 463 pp.
    Refers to women's participation in more than a dozen different places, all identified in the index. Includes such topics as women's clubs, bicycling, and women's role in nineteenth- and twentieth-century sports.

2   FOREMAN, KEN, and HUSTED, VIRGINIA. *Track and Field Techniques for Girls and Women*. Dubuque, Iowa: William C. Brown Co., 209 pp.
    Provides principles and performance techniques for each track and field event. Includes a section on mechanical principles and motor learning theory related to track and field. Provides suggested training schedules for both beginning and advanced performers in most events; includes information on general conditioning.

3   GALLICO, PAUL. *The Golden People*. Garden City, N.Y.: Doubleday & Co., 315 pp.
    Includes biographical sketches for Gertrude Ederle (pp. 46-65), Helen Wills (pp. 154-175), and Babe Didrikson (pp. 234-251). Written in the inimitable style of Gallico and presents his personal view of these three athletes.

4   HORAN, RUTH. *Judo for Women*. New York: Crown Publishers, 158 pp.
    Designed as a basic self-defense text for women; includes a brief history of judo and detailed analyses of judo techniques, all of which are illustrated with photographs.

5   HUMISTON, DOROTHY, and MICHEL, DOROTHY. *Fundamentals of Sports for Girls and Women*. New York: The Ronald Press Co., 217 pp.
    Analyzes skills and strategies for six team sports and five individual/dual sports as well as teaching hints and practice formations for each of the sports. Includes specific instructions for left-handed players.

6   METHENY, ELEANOR. "On Women and Sport." In *Connotations of Movement in Sport and Dance*. Dubuque, Iowa: William C. Brown Co., pp. 129-219.

Presents a collection of eight essays concerned with women and sport originally presented as speeches by Metheny to varying audiences. Topics range from folklore, fiction, and fantasy about women in sport to examining the future of women's sport.

7   POSTAL, BERNARD; SILVER, JESSE; and SILVER, ROY. *Encyclopedia of Jews in Sport*. New York: Bloch Publishing Co., 539 pp.

Compiled in encyclopedic form and arranged alphabetically by sport. Includes a number of women ranging from auto racers to track and field athletes; provides brief biographical sketches for each.

8   SMITH, MARGARET. *The Margaret Smith Story*. London: Stanley Paul, 192 pp.

Describes Smith's early introduction to tennis as a child in Australia, her climb up the ladder of success, and the trials and tribulations encountered along the way. She concludes her autobiography with instructional tips for women players.

9   TROTTER, BETTY JANE. *Volleyball for Girls and Women*. New York: Ronald Press Co., 237 pp.

Outlines the history of volleyball and benefits of the game to players. Presents individual skill analysis and team patterns of play. Offers suggestions for teaching the game, organizing intramural play, and developing competitive programs.

10   VANNIER, MARYHELEN. *A Better Figure for You through Exercise and Diet*. New York: Association Press, 128 pp.

Focuses on nutrition and exercise as a way of developing a desirable figure. Includes specific exercises for various body parts, relaxation techniques, and clues for managing time in order to engage in physical activities.

1966

1   BARNES, MILDRED J.; FOX, MARGARET G.; SCOTT, M. GLADYS; and LOEFFLER, PAULINE A. *Sports Activities for Girls and Women*. New York: Appleton-Century-Crofts, 500 pp.

Designed for the would-be learner of sport skills; includes instructional analyses for eighteen different activities. Common errors and corrections for them are provided for each activity.

2   BELL, PEGGY KIRK. *A Woman's Way to Better Golf*. New York: E.P. Dutton & Co., 128 pp.

Uses provocative chapter titles (Choose Your Weapons, Mind Your Manners, Sweeping with a Wood, Lady Drivers Can Be Good) to lead the reader through the intricacies of learning how to play golf. Analyzes and illustrates the necessary skills for game play; concludes with "advice to the lovelorn," final tips for those who have fallen in love with the game.

3   MEADE, GEORGE P. "Swimming Records, Women Swimmers Versus Men." In *Athletic Records, the Whys and Wherefores*. New York: Vantage Press, pp. 81-94.

Compares men's early swim records with those being achieved by women in 1965.

4   NEAL, PATSY. *Basketball Techniques for Women*. New York: Ronald Press Co., 233 pp.

Clarifies the status of women's six-player basketball in 1966 with an explanation of the rules in use, a four-player offense and four-player defense, using two players who are allowed to "rove" or play the full court. Includes individual skill techniques and team strategy for playing the game. Concludes with a chapter on basketball for the highly skilled and outlines the competitive opportunities available to women.

5   SCHAAFSMA, FRANCES. *Women's Basketball*. Dubuque, Iowa: William C. Brown Co., 70 pp.

Written as a text for use in college classes. Includes basic skills, techniques, strategies, and rules for the six-player game, using a four-player offense and four-player defense with two players allowed to "rove" the full court. Questions for self-evaluation are distributed throughout the book.

6   WAKEFIELD, FRANCES; HARKINS, DOROTHY; with COOPER, JOHN M. *Track and Field Fundamentals for Girls and Women*. St. Louis: C.V. Mosby Co., 263 pp.

Analyzes performance techniques for each track and field event, including distance running; notes, for the latter, that 1500 meters and one and one half miles are the longest distances used in competition. Planning and managing aspects for conducting a competitive meet are presented. Provides suggestions for improvising equipment for track and field if none is available for women. Training programs, suggested lesson plans, and meet results for elementary school girls are found in appendixes.

1968

1   CONNOLLY, OLGA. *The Rings of Destiny*. New York: David McKay Co., 311 pp.

Describes the personal story of the Olympic romance between Czechoslovakian discus thrower Olga Fikotova, and United States hammer thrower Harold Connolly, which culminated in their marriage after special permission was granted by the Czechoslovakian government.

2   COOPER, PHYLLIS. *Feminine Gymnastics*. Minneapolis: Burgess Publishing Co., 204 pp.

Provides methods, evaluation techniques, and safety procedures for teaching gymnastics. Includes skill analysis for apparatus performance and suggestions for composing gymnastic routines.

3   GIBSON, ALTHEA, and CURTIS, RICHARD. *So Much To Live For*. New York: G.P. Putnam's Sons, 160 pp.

Details Gibson's life after her retirement from amateur tennis at the peak of her career. Describes her stint as an actress and singer, presenting tennis exhibitions, traveling with the Harlem Globetrotters, and her eventual entry into professional golf.

4   HENDERSON, EDWIN B. *The Black Athlete: Emergence and Arrival.* New York: Publishers Co., 329 pp.

Includes brief biographical sketches for tennis player Althea Gibson (pp. 268-271), and runners Wilma Rudolph (pp. 262-263) and Wyomia Tyus (pp. 263-265).

5   LOWRY, CARLA. *Pictorial Basketball for Women.* Hollywood, Calif.: Creative Sports Books, 38 pp.

Presents a collection of action photos of women basketball players; demonstrates beginning and advanced skills such as passing, dribbling, and shooting.

6   MORIN, NEA. *A Woman's Reach, Mountaineering Memoirs.* New York: Dodd, Mead & Co., 288 pp.

Vividly describes the challenge of the mountains in a personal account of Morin's long and remarkable climbing career. Describes her major climbs from 1922 to 1959, when her serious climbing was curtailed because of osteoarthritis. The elation and exhilaration often voiced by climbers is evident in Morin's record of her long involvement with climbing.

7   VANNIER, MARYHELEN, and POINDEXTER, HALL B.W. *Individual and Team Sports for Girls and Women,* 2d ed. Philadelphia: W.B. Saunders Co., 643 pp.

Expands information from the first edition (4) and omits the novelty events and techniques included in 1960.

1969

1   BARNES, MILDRED J. *Field Hockey, the Coach and the Player.* Boston: Allyn & Bacon, 272 pp.

Covers almost every aspect needed for playing, teaching, or coaching field hockey. Presents skill analysis, game strategy, practice suggestions, rainy-day ideas, introducing the game to beginners, facilities and equipment, and coaching techniques.

2   BRYANT, CAROL A. *Hockey for Schools.* London: Pelman Books, 164 pp.

Presents analysis of individual techniques; describes team strategy. Includes umpiring techniques, tournament organization, equipment needed, and maintenance of grounds. A special feature is the emphasis on choosing the right movement at the right time in game play.

3   CARTER, ERNESTINE RUSSELL. *Gymnastics for Girls and Women*. Englewood Cliffs, N.J.: Prentice-Hall, 217 pp.

Designed for the gymnastics teacher; analyzes the skills most commonly performed in floor exercise, vaulting, on the balance beam and the uneven bars. Provides techniques for spotting, suggestions on points of form and judging performance, and details for conducting a gymnastics meet.

4   COCHRANE, TUOVI SAPPINEN. *International Gymnastics for Girls and Women*. Reading, Mass.: Addison-Wesley Publishing Co., 248 pp.

Contains most of the information needed for the gymnastics teacher to begin a program. Includes skill analysis for women's four competitive events, uneven bars, balance beam, floor exercise, and vaulting. Includes instructions for gymnastics with instruments and hand apparatus, developmental exercises, and gymnastic routines. Sample lessons are provided for some of the activities.

5   JACKSON, NELL. *Track and Field for Girls and Women*. Minneapolis: Burgess Publishing Co., 143 pp.

Utilizes the author's past experiences and knowledge as a former Olympic competitor and coach in analyzing the major track and field events of running, throwing, and jumping. Illustrates mechanical principles with photographs and drawings; provides information on condition and training, warming up, and organizing a track and field meet.

6   JOSEY, MARTHA, with PATTIE, JANE. *Fundamentals of Barrel Racing*. Houston: Cordovan Corp., 89 pp.

Written in language for beginning learners; offers the necessary information for learning the sport of barrel racing which is performed only by women at the professional level, and primarily by women at the amateur level. Provides advice for selecting the right barrel horse, equipment, and costume. Includes information about conditioning, training, and seasoning (working in different arenas) the horse; techniques for horse and rider; and riding in competition.

7   KJELDSEN, KITTY. *Women's Gymnastics*. Boston: Allyn & Bacon, 96 pp.

Combines a simplified analysis of basic skills with a movement-exploration approach to aid learners in mastering beginning gymnastics skills. Identifies key concepts around which gymnastics is structured; suggests learning experiences for developing specific outcomes.

8   LEES, JOSEPHINE T. and SHELLENBERGER, JOSEPHINE. *Field Hockey*. Hanover, N.H.: ABK Publications, 153 pp.

Discusses equipment, individual skill analysis, team tactics, umpiring, duties of players, and practice procedures; focuses primarily on teaching. Includes a lengthy glossary of field hockey terms.

9   McCUE, BETTY FOSTER. *Physical Activities for Women*. New York: The Macmillan Co., 421 pp.

Designed as a supplementary reader to assist in the learning of sports skills. Generally includes a brief history, necessary equipment, résumé of rules, skill analysis, etiquette, and safety practices for nineteen different activities. Introductory chapters focus on the values of exercise and basic principles of body mechanics.

10 NEAL, PATSY. *Coaching Methods for Women*. Reading, Mass.: Addison-Wesley Publishing Co., 294 pp.

Written primarily for coaches of girls' and women's sports; includes information on the role of the coach, factors in coaching women, and prerequisites for the development of champions. Discusses the practical aspects of coaching such as organizing and selecting a team, training and conditioning, and planning for the sports season. Analyzes skills and strategies for twelve sports including coaching suggestions for each. Basketball, Neal's sport, is not included. Offers diverse information about the coaching of women, and Neal's own philosophy of coaching permeates the narrative.

11 PARKER, VIRGINIA, and KENNEDY, ROBERT. *Track and Field for Girls and Women*. Philadelphia: W.B. Saunders Co., 127 pp.

Written for the beginning performer in track and field who wishes to learn basic skills or improve performance by correcting common errors; analyzes fundamental skills for all events including middle-distance and cross-country running; offers suggestions for training and conditioning, safety precautions, and rules for women's events.

12 SCHREIBER, MARY L. *Women's Gymnastics*. Pacific Palisades, Calif.: Goodyear Publishing Co., 88 pp.

Presents basic skill analysis for each of the major gymnastic events for women; includes conditioning exercises for the sport. Illustrated with sequence photographs.

13 STUTTS, ANN. *Women's Basketball*. Pacific Palisades, Calif.: Goodyear Publishing Co., 80 pp.

Devoted primarily to techniques for playing the six-player game. Skills and strategies are analyzed; includes a brief history of the women's game and a synopsis of rules.

14 THOMPSON, DONNIS H. *Women's Track and Field*. Boston: Allyn & Bacon, 96 pp.

Designed as a self-instruction manual for women's track and field. Identifies major concepts for each women's event with selected learning experiences leading to an understanding of those concepts.

15 VANNIER, MARYHELEN, and POINDEXTER, HALLY B.W. *Physical Activities for College Women*, 2d ed. Philadelphia: W.B. Saunders Co., 631 pp.

Expands the first edition published in 1964 (10) to include a discussion of the physiological benefits of exercise. Added new exercises on figure and weight control and a new chapter on surfing. Rules for sports are updated.

16 WEISS, PAUL. "Women and Men: A Philosophical Inquiry." In *Sport: A Philosophic Inquiry*. Carbondale: Southern Illinois University Press, pp. 181-193.

Makes a philosophical comparison of women's and men's involvement in sport. In general, attempts to explain the lack of success women have achieved in the sport world.

1970

1   BURKE, JOHN. *Winged Legend: The Story of Amelia Earhart*. New York: G.P. Putnam's Sons, 255 pp.
     Details Earhart's early life and career as a flyer, including descriptions of her major flights.

2   DELANO, ANNE LEE. *Lacrosse for Girls and Women*. Dubuque, Iowa: Willam C. Brown Co., 76 pp.
     Designed as a basic instructional manual; includes skill techniques, requirements for team positions, fundamental offensive and defensive play, and a summary of rules. Briefly traces the history of lacrosse.

3   GUSTUSON, DONALD L. and MASAKI, LINDA. *Self-Defense for Women*. Boston: Allyn & Bacon, 80 pp.
     Designed for use in instructional classes or by the self-learner; utilizes a conceptual approach in presenting material for learning. Basic concepts are followed by related information and practice situations for developing the appropriate skills and knowledge necessary for defending oneself.

4   HELMKER, JUDITH. *High School Girls' Athletic Associations*. New York: A.S. Barnes & Co., 339 pp.
     Focuses on the development of athletic programs for girls that are organized within the school, primarily in the form of intramurals supplemented with play days and sport days with other schools. Includes organizational procedures, program values, policy development, administration, and public relations. Minimal attention is given to interscholastic competition.

5   HEYDEN, MARGARET S. and TARPENNING, ALLAN. *Personal Defense for Women*. Belmont, Calif.: Wadsworth Publishing Co., 94 pp.

Describes basic techniques for self-defense in a variety of situations. Discusses equipment such as a comb or nail file which might be available to a woman for defending herself. Includes safety precautions to avoid problems, legal implications of defense, and training techniques for keeping in shape.

6 HAUSSERMANN, CAROLINE. *Field Hockey*. Boston: Allyn & Bacon, 77 pp.

Presents the basic fundamentals of field hockey; uses a conceptual approach in developing the instructional materials; provides experiences for learning the concepts selected.

7 MILLER, KENNETH D., and HORKY, RITA J. *Modern Basketball for Women*. Columbus, Ohio: Charles E. Miller Publishing Co., 190 pp.

Presents a brief history of women's basketball, including a section on international competition. Includes techniques for both the five- and six-player games. Analyzes fundamental skills of basketball; describes basic offensive and defensive strategies; offers suggestions for problems which may be encountered by the beginning coach.

8 PRICE, LA FERNE ELLIS. *The Wonder of Motion: A Sense of Life for Women*. Grand Forks: University of North Dakota Press, 79 pp.

Explores the emotional element of woman's involvement in sport. Both verbal images in the form of free verse and artistic illustrations are used to portray women in a variety of sports. Is essentially a book of introspection, an effort to describe the inner feelings of the female as she engages in sporting activities.

9 SPENCER, HELEN. *Beginning Field Hockey*. Belmont, Calif.: Wadsworth Publishing Co., 61 pp.

Written for beginning players; includes a brief history of field hockey, rules for play, and analysis of individual skills. Describes techniques for self-testing and evaluation.

10 *Sports Programs for College Women*. Washington, D.C.: American Association for Health, Physical Education, and Recreation, 70 pp.

Examines the status of college women's sports, suggesting potential directions for such programs. Includes essays representing the broad topical areas of ethics and values; programs, problems, directions; and interrelationships with other sports organizations.

11 WAKEFIELD, FRANCES; HARKINS, DOROTHY; with COOPER, JOHN M. *Track and Field Fundamentals for Girls and Women*, 2d ed. St. Louis: C.V. Mosby Co., 274 pp.

Originally published in 1966 (6); sections on the pentathlon and how to begin a track and field program have been added. Skill analysis has been re vised and records updated.

1971

1 BROER, MARION R., ed. *Individual Sports for Women*, Philadelphia: W. B. Saunders Co., 386 pp.

Developed for use as an instructional manual for individual sports; includes a section on principles of learning. Covers archery, badminton, bowling, fencing, golf, riding, swimming, and tennis. Skill analysis, suggested lessons, organizational techniques, and recommended equipment are presented for each activity. A bibliography for further reading is included for each sport, and for some activities, audiovisual materials are listed.

2 DAVIDSON, OWEN, and JONES, C. M. *Great Women Tennis Players*. London: Pelham Books, 142 pp.

Presents brief sketches of the tennis playing careers of women champions ranging from early greats, Charlotte Cooper, Charlotte Dod (the youngest singles Wimbledon champion in history at the age of fifteen), and Dorothea Douglas Chambers, seventeen-time Wimbledon champion, to Maria Bueno, Margaret Court, and Billie Jean King. Includes "isolated mortals" Cilli Aussem, Lili d'Alvarez, Molla Mallory, and Dorothy Round. Focuses on the tennis feats of the individual players with particular reference to their wins at Wimbledon.

3 DOBSON, MARGARET J., and SISLEY, BECKY L. *Softball for Girls*. New York: Ronald Press Co., 224 pp.

Written for teachers and coaches of softball; covers all phases of the game from basic skill analysis to advanced playing and coaching techniques. Provides evaluation techniques, indoor and outdoor practice situations, and suggestions for elementary, secondary, and college programs. Includes a detailed bibliography for additional sources of information and a list of visual aids.

4   FOREMAN, KEN, and HUSTED, VIRGINIA. *Track and Field Techniques for Girls and Women*, 2d ed. Dubuque, Iowa: William C. Brown Co., 291 pp.,
        Originally published in 1965 (2); practical hints for competitor and coach based on research findings have been added. Includes two chapters on long distance running and new information on conditioning regarding the use of weights.

5   GARDNER, RUTH. *Judo for the Gentle Woman*. Rutland, Vt.: C.E. Tuttle Co., 147 pp.
        Designed as a "how-to-do-it" book; includes the basic fundamentals of judo with analyses of falls, self-defense techniques, and basic throwing techniques. Stresses the importance of a competent instructor in actual practice and for progressing to more advanced skills.

6   HARRIS, DOROTHY V. *DGWS Research Reports: Women in Sport*, vol. 1. Washington, D.C.: American Association for Health, Physical Education, and Recreation, 110 pp.
        Contains articles by fifteen different authors who present syntheses of completed research on the female sports participant. Excellent bibliographies accompany most of the articles, and information is included on the psychosocial, physiological, and teaching and coaching aspects of women in sport.

7   HIGDON, HAL. *Champions of the Tennis Court*. Englewood Cliffs, N.J.: Prentice-Hall, 60 pp.
        Presents brief biographical sketches of four women tennis champions in a collection of eleven minibiographies. Highlights the careers of Suzanne Lenglen, Helen Wills, Maureen Connolly, and Billie Jean King.

8   HUGHES, ERIC LESTER. *Gymnastics for Girls: A Competitive Approach for Teacher and Coach*, 2d ed. New York: Ronald Press Co., 275 pp.

Expands the first edition published in 1963 (1). Considers recent trends in the sport and has added or changed routines to incorporate them. Includes a section on modern gymnastics using apparatus such as hoops and balls.

9   JOHNSON, BARRY L., and BOUDREAUX, PATRICIA D. *Basic Gymnastics for Girls and Women*. New York: Appleton-Century-Crofts, 130 pp.

Designed as a book for beginning learners or teachers of beginning gymnastics classes. Presents instructions for approximately 100 stunts; offers suggestions for class organization and evaluating and grading students.

10   JONES, ANN. *A Game to Love*. London: Stanley Paul, 192 pp.

Details the life and tennis career of the author from recollections of her early childhood to her successful win at Wimbledon in 1969.

11   LITTLEWOOD, MARY. *Women's Softball*. Chicago: Athletic Institute, 76 pp.

Describes the fundamental skills needed for playing fast-pitch softball; outlines the special responsibilities of infield and outfield players. Illustrated with photographs and diagrams; concludes with a detailed glossary of softball terms for the beginning player.

12   MILLER, DONNA MAE, and RUSSELL, KATHRYN R.E. "Sport and Women." In *Sport: A Contemporary View*. Philadelphia: Lea and Febiger, pp. 116-145.

Focuses on "what sociologists would label as a microcosm of the larger society–women in sport" (p. 116). Examines the role of women's sports in relation to cultural expectations; concludes with a section on equality of opportunity.

13   MORAN, SHARRON. *Golf is a Woman's Game*. New York: Hawthorn Books, 202 pp.

Analyzes and illustrates with photographs the techniques of driving and putting the golf ball; offers suggestions for dealing with difficult shots. Describes each of the clubs and their uses; analyzes common performance problems and provides suggestions for improvement.

14   PATERSON, ANN, and WEST, EULA, eds. *Team Sports for Girls*, 2d ed. New York: Ronald Press Co., 362 pp.

First published in 1959 (5); designed as an instructional manual for teaching team sports to girls. Includes basketball, field hockey, lacrosse, soccer, speedball, speed-a-way, and volleyball. General information about the teaching of team sports is presented followed by separate chapters that include history and purpose of the game, necessary facilities and equipment, analysis of game skills, techniques of team strategy, and a suggested teaching progression.

15   SCHAAFSMA, FRANCES. *Women's Basketball*, 2d ed. Dubuque, Iowa: William C. Brown Co., 71 pp.

Originally published in 1966 (5); defensive and offensive strategies have been altered to accommodate the five-player, full court game of basketball.

16   SCHAAFSMA, FRANCES, and HECK, ANN. *Volleyball for Coaches and Teachers*. Dubuque, Iowa: William C. Brown Publishers, 162 pp.

Designed for teachers and coaches; offers detailed analyses of volleyball skills; thoroughly explains offensive and defensive strategies. Includes suggestions for training, conditioning, and injury prevention. Presents an overview of factors affecting learning with suggestions for application to volleyball coaching. Outlines administrative procedures for conducting a volleyball program.

17   UNDERHILL, MIRIAM. *Give Me the Hills*. Riverside, Conn.: Chatham Press, 278 pp.

Presents a personal account of the author's love affair with the mountains. Describes her mountaineering exploits that spanned over forty years and ranged over peaks in both Europe and the United States. Describes her pioneering efforts in "manless" climbing with no male guides and winter climbs in the New Hampshire four thousand footers. Numerous photographs appear throughout the book, contributing to the feeling of joyful adventure that pervades the text.

1972

1   BARNES, MILDRED. *Women's Basketball*. Boston: Allyn & Bacon, 341 pp.

   Provides detailed analysis of individual skills and offensive and defensive strategies for the five-player game of basketball. Includes teaching progressions, suggestions for class organization, and ideas for coaches working with competitive teams.

2   BOWERS, CAROLYN O.; FIE, JACQUELYN U.; KJELDSEN, KITTY; and SCHMID, ANDREA B. *Judging and Coaching Women's Gymnastics*. Palo Alto, Calif.: National Press Books, 217 pp.

   Structured as a practical guide to provide gymnastics judges with a technical understanding of gymnastic skills and aid them in making the critical decisions necessary for judging competition. Describes correct technique and common technical errors for each event and specific penalties and deductions resulting in loss of points. Includes psychology of coaching and philosophy of judging and coaching gymnastics.

3   COOPER, MILDRED, and COOPER, KENNETH H. *Aerobics for Women*. New York: Bantam Books, 160 pp.

   Based on Kenneth Cooper's well-known program of physical fitness for men, but designed specifically for women's use. Includes a series of suggested exercise programs for various age levels, recommended tests for determining the level of physical conditioning, warm-up procedures prior to exercise, and suggestions for combining diet with exercise. Written in a friendly, conversational style.

4   EBERT, FRANCES H., and CHEATUM, BILLYE ANN. *Basketball – Five Player*. Philadelphia: W.B. Saunders Co., 287 pp.

   Written to aid in the transition from the six to five-player game for women. Analyzes individual skills and team strategies; includes sections on conditioning for basketball, treatment of athletic injuries, and suggestions for coaching competitive teams. Outlines major rules changes since 1907 and briefly sketches the history of basketball.

5 GOULD, SHIRLEY. *Swimming the Shane Gould Way*. New York: Sterling Publishing Co., 160 pp.

   Contains a wide range of information about swimming and the competitive swimmer. Analyzes the freestyle, breaststroke, butterfly, and backstroke as performed by Shane Gould; provides training and conditioning techniques and the fine points of racing competition. In a more personal vein, explores other aspects of swimming competition such as the relationship between parents, coach, and swimmer.

6 GRIMSLEY, WILL, ed. *The Sports Immortals*. Englewood Cliffs, N.J.: Prentice-Hall, 320 pp.

   Includes three women among those persons identified as the greatest athletes in the history of modern sports. Biographies for Helen Wills Moody, Sonja Henie, and Babe Didrikson Zaharias sketch the highlights of their careers and provide an indication of why they are considered sports immortals.

7 HASS, LOTTE. *Girl on the Ocean Floor*. London: George C. Harrap & Co., 166 pp.

   Vividly describes Hass's experiences as the only woman to accompany a 1949 expedition to make the first dives in the shark-infested Red Sea for the purpose of making an underwater film. Lotte Beierl begins as a secretary to Hans Hass, well-known underwater diver, and is allowed to go on the expedition primarily to keep records and do the "housekeeping chores," but soon proves herself to be an accomplished diver and photographer. Provides descriptive accounts of the many unusual events that occurred on the expedition, which culminated in a prize-winning film and Beierl's marriage to Hass.

8 HOLBROOK, LEONA. "Women's Participation in American Sport." In *Athletics in America*. Edited by Arnold Flath. Corvallis: Oregon University Press, pp. 43-59.

   Offers a brief overview of the historical involvement of women in sports, identifies current problems and areas in which further research is needed.

9   HOLLANDER, PHYLLIS. *American Women in Sports*. New York: Grossett and Dunlap, 112 pp.

Presents more than fifty brief sketches of American sportswomen in nine different activities. Selections range from such early champions as Eleanora Sears, Stella Walsh, Glenna Collett, and Gertrude Ederle to those of more recent years, Billie Jean King, Peggy Fleming, Kathy Whitworth, and Debbie Meyer. A separate chapter highlights the diverse career of Babe Didrikson Zaharias. Sports heroines from bowling, riding, tennis, swimming and diving, track and field, figure skating, golf, skiing, and channel swimming are included.

10   LOWRY, CARLA. *Women's Basketball*. Chicago: Athletic Institute, 68 pp.

Describes techniques and strategies for playing basketball, using numerous photographs to illustrate the information covered in the text.

11   OFFSTEIN, JERROLD. *Self-defense for Women*. Palo Alto, Calif.: National Press Books, 76 pp.

Uses elements and techniques from karate, jiujitsu, judo, and aikido to develop a progressive series of skills for practical self-defense. Tactics are designed primarily for repelling sexual assaults. Includes a lengthy discussion of history, philosophy, and principles of karate.

12   TAYLOR, BRYCE; BAJIN, BORIS; and ZIVIC, TOM. *Olympic Gymnastics for Men and Women*. Englewood Cliffs, N.J.: Prentice-Hall, 239 pp.

Focuses on the development of gymnasts as high level competitors. Includes selection of performers; analyzes skills for each of the areas in which women and men compete.

13   WARREN, MEG. *The Book of Gymnastics*. London: Arthur Baker, 113 pp.

Describes technique and style for performing basic skills in the major gymnastic events for women. Focuses on beginning work in gymnastics.

1973

1 BELL, MARY M. *Women's Basketball*, 2d ed. Dubuque, Iowa: William C. Brown Co., 143 pp.

Originally published in 1964 (2); offensive and defensive strategies have been altered to accommodate the five-player full court game for women rather than the six-player half court game. Suggestions for coaching competitive teams are expanded to reflect the growing programs of collegiate competition in basketball.

2 BUTLER, HAL. "Gertrude Ederle, the Girl Who Didn't Have a Chance." In *Sports Heroes Who Wouldn't Quit*. New York: Julian Messner, pp. 167-176.

Briefly traces Ederle's life and swimming career. Focuses on her English Channel swim in 1926, the first woman to succeed with the swim.

3 COOPER, PHYLLIS. *Feminine Gymnastics*, 2d ed. Minneapolis: Burgess Publishing Co., 269 pp.

Expands the 1968 edition (2) to reflect the increasing interest in gymnastics competition and the variety of skills being performed in gymnastics meets.

4 COYNE, JOHN, ed. *The New Golf for Women*. New York: Doubleday & Co., 223 pp.

Presents information about golf written by professional golfers considered outstanding in the areas about which they write. Kathy Whitworth analyzes fundamental skills. Betty Burfeindt discusses driving for distance; Judy Rankin, playing the woods; Sandra Haynie, playing the long irons; Sandy Palmer, playing the short irons; and Mary Mills, playing the wedge. Putting is analyzed by Pam Barnett; Jane Blalock offers advice for playing trouble shots. Generously illustrated with photographs of the authors.

5 DRURY, BLANCHE JESSEN, and SCHMID, ANDREA B. *Introduction to Women's Gymnastics*. Palo Alto, Calif.: National Press Books, 112 pp.

Written primarily for the beginning gymnastics student and the secondary school teacher. Analyzes skills for each of the competitive events, balance beam, uneven bars, floor exercise, and vaulting and basic tumbling and dance moves. Includes a skills progression check list for the four competitive events.

6   HANEY, LYNN. *The Lady Is a Jock*. New York: Dodd, Mead & Co., 180 pp.

Details the gypsy life of the female jockey; describes the careers of Barbara Jo Rubin, the first woman jockey to rise to fame; Robyn Smith, who left a potential acting career to follow the track; Patty Barton, who began her career as a saddle bronc rider; and the often controversial Mary Bacon, whose unusual antics both off and on the track frequently resulted in news sensationalism. Highlights some of the lesser known women jockeys and comments briefly on several women who hold other posts as trainer, veterinarian, agent, groom, exercise girl, and valet in the racing profession. Explores the reasons women may choose professional careers in racing and some of the psychological aspects of women's interest in horses.

7   HARRIS, DOROTHY V. *DGWS Research Reports: Women in Sport*, vol. 2. Washington, D.C.: American Association for Health, Physical Education, and Recreation, 153 pp.

Presents a collection of articles synthesizing recent research on women in sport. Information is included on the biomechanical, physiological, and psychological aspects of the female sports participant with bibliographies accompanying most of the articles.

8   _____. "Compatibility of Femininity and Athletic Involvement." In *Involvement in Sport: A Somatopsychic Rationale for Physical Activity*. Philadelphia: Lea & Febiger, pp. 192-209.

Discusses the physiological and psychological misconceptions about female athletes and the cultural restrictions on athletic participation.

9   MUSHIER, CAROLE L. *Team Sports for Girls and Women*. Dubuque, Iowa: William C. Brown and Co., 219 pp.

Focuses on teaching techniques for the team sports commonly included as activities in physical education programs for girls and women: basketball, field hockey, lacrosse, soccer, speedball, speed-a-way, softball, and volleyball. General information on principles of learning applied to team sports precedes the chapters on specific techniques for each sport. Skill analysis, team strategy, necessary equipment, and a unit plan of instruction for beginning players are included for each activity.

10   POINDEXTER, HALLY B.W., and MUSHIER, CAROLE L. *Coaching Competitive Team Sports for Girls and Women.* Philadelphia: W.B. Saunders Co., 257 pp.

Provides an overall view of information needed by coaches of women's team sports. An introductory chapter defines the role of competition, its purposes, objectives, and values for women. Subsequent chapters provide practical information concerning the organization and administration of a competitive program and guidelines for team selection and practice sessions. Separate chapters on basketball, field hockey, lacrosse, softball, and volleyball provide specific suggestions for coaching these sports including player selection, advanced skills necessary for competitive play, team strategy, suggestions for practice sessions, and coaching during game play.

11   SCOTT, EUGENE. *Tennis: A Game of Motion.* New York: Crown Publishers, 256 pp.

Devotes about half of the information to women including a gallery of action photographs with little narrative. Provides brief sketches and photographs of Helen Wills, Suzanne Lenglen, Maureen Connolly, Margaret Court, Evonne Goolagong, Chris Evert, and Billie Jean King. A concluding chapter details the historic matches between Lenglen and Wills in 1926 and Goolagong and Evert in 1971. Other sections include photographs of women players, candid shots of unknown players as well as the best-known champions of the game.

12   STAMBLER, IRWIN. *Speed Kings: World's Fastest Humans.* New York: Doubleday & Co., 162 pp.

Includes a selection of twelve of the "world's fastest humans," two of whom are women. Provides a brief biographical sketch of Chi Cheng (pp. 1-13), first Asian woman to win an Olympic medal, outlines her running career, and describes in detail her record-breaking run of ten seconds in the 100-yard dash in 1970. A section on Shane Gould (pp. 27-39) focuses on her 1972 100-meter freestyle performance of 58.5 seconds, which made her the swimming world's fastest woman.

13   STEPHENS, WILL. *Women's Track and Field*. Chicago: Athletic Institute, 92 pp.

Outlines performance analysis for each of the track and field events in which women participate; fully illustrated with photographs. Includes diet suggestions for track athletes and a summary of rules.

14   STUTTS, ANN. *Women's Basketball*, 2d ed. Pacific Palisades, Calif.: Goodyear Publishing Co., 82 pp.

Originally published in 1969 (13). Second edition alters offensive and defensive strategy to accommodate the five-player, full court basketball game.

15   *Tennis for Women*. New York: Doubleday & Co., 256 pp.

Contains a collection of treatises on the various aspects of tennis written by players from the Women's Pro Tour. Includes sections on all skills, court strategy, doubles and mixed doubles play, and conditioning techniques for tennis.

16   THOMPSON, DONNIS H. *Modern Track and Field for Girls and Women*. Boston: Allyn & Bacon, 288 pp.

Presents the mechanical principles of performance for each of the major track and field events. Includes common errors and corrections, a teaching progression, and rules that govern participation in each event. Offers planning suggestions for teaching and coaching track and field, and organizational and administrative procedures for planning meets.

17   TURNBULL, ANNE E. *Basketball for Women*, Reading, Mass.: Addison-Wesley Publishing Co., 218 pp.

Contains skill analyses and descriptions of offensive and defensive strategy; focuses primarily on facets of the game for use by coaches of competitive teams. Includes information on administrative procedures, conditioning, prevention of athletic injuries, and psychological aspects of coaching.

18   WAKEFIELD, FRANCES; HARKINS, DOROTHY; with COOPER, JOHN M. *Track and Field Fundamentals for Girls and Women*. St. Louis: C. V. Mosby Co., 311 pp.

Originally published in 1966 (6), revised in 1970 (11). Third edition updates information based on current knowledge.

19   WEIR, MARIE. *Women's Hockey for the Seventies*. London: Kaye & Ward, 190 pp.

Provides information concerning skill performance and game strategy; includes principles of play, game psychology, suggestions for coaching, and a look at the future of hockey for women.

20   WILLIAMS, CICELY. *Women on the Rope*. London: George Allen & Unwin, 240 pp.

Presents a descriptive history of women's participation in mountain climbing. Colorful accounts of nineteenth-century women, the "petticoat pioneers" who climbed in long dresses and crinoline petticoats, are followed by the feats of seasoned climbers of the twentieth century such as Yvette Vaucher, the first woman included in a Mt. Everest expedition.

1974

1   BAKER, JIM. *Billie Jean King*. New York: Grosset & Dunlap Publishers, 90 pp.

Describes King's early life and amateur career; devotes a major portion of the narrative to her activities in professional tennis and her work as a player-coach with World Team Tennis. Relates her views on women's rights and her efforts to gain equity for women in tennis. Includes a chronological list of all of King's major championships through 1974.

2   BARNES, MILDRED J. *Girls' Basketball*. New York: Sterling Publishing Co., 144 pp.

Describes the five-player basketball game; presents analysis of individual skills, offensive and defensive strategy, and a summary of playing rules.

3   BEECHAM, JUSTIN. *Olga, Her Life and Her Gymnastics*. New York: Two Continents Publishing Groups, 128 pp.

Focuses on the life and gymnastic career of Olga Korbut; presents an abbreviated history of the development of gymnastics and its place in the Olympic Games.

4   BETTS, JOHN RICKARDS. "Feminine Approval and Public Recognition." In *America's Sporting Heritage: 1850-1950*. Reading, Mass.: Addison-Wesley Publishing Co., pp. 218-231.

Focuses primarily on the acceptance of sport in American culture and women's role in that acceptance. Other brief references to women's sport participation between 1850 and 1950 are scattered throughout the book.

5   BOSLOOPER, THOMAS, & HAYES, MARCIA. *The Femininity Game*. New York: Stein & Day, 227 pp.

Analyzes societal expectations of the female, particularly in relation to the development of athletic skill. Discusses physiological and psychological biases that have deterred women from entering the world of sport or pursuing success as a sportswoman after a certain age. Offers suggestions to overcome prevailing biases, and reviews briefly some of the progress that has been made in providing opportunities in sport participation for women.

6   GERBER, ELLEN W.; FELSHIN, JAN; BERLIN, PEARL; and WYRICK, WANEEN. *The American Woman in Sport*. Reading, Mass.: Addison-Wesley Publishing Co., 573 pp.

Provides an analysis of the American woman in sport with information limited to females of college age or older. Explores the role of woman in sport within specific boundaries: the historical development of sport for women; the sportswoman in the context of society; psychological dimensions of the woman in sport; and the biophysical factors of the female as they relate to her participation in sport. Each section concludes with an extensive bibliography.

7   HOEPNER, BARBARA J., ed. *Women's Athletics: Coping with Controversy*. Washington, D.C.: American Association for Health, Physical Education, and Recreation, 120 pp.

Includes the presentations of fourteen speakers who dealt with the topic, "Women's Athletics," at the 1973 convention of the American Association for Health, Physical Education, and Recreation and two papers from the 1973 National Coaches Conference. Section headings include "Overview of Women's Rights;" "Women's Intercollegiate Athletics Past, Present, Future;" "The Olympic Games;" "Women in Athletics;" and "Welfare of Women in Sports." The speakers represent a broad range of interests from teachers, researchers, and administrators to coaches and Olympic athletes, and the papers are a reflection of the diverse views of such a group.

8   JACOBS, LINDA. *Chris Evert: Tennis Pro*. St. Paul: EMC Corp., 40 pp.

Provides an overview of the life and career of tennis player, Chris Evert. Emphasizes Evert's determination to be herself and the personal characteristics which gave her the name, "Little Miss Cool." Focuses primarily on her career after becoming a professional at the age of eighteen.

9   _____. *Janet Lynn: Sunshine on Ice*. St. Paul: EMC Corp., 40 pp.

Describes Lynn's introduction to figure skating at the age of two and a half; follows her career to her joining the professional ranks at the age of twenty. Captures her "sunshine" personality while emphasizing the importance of her strong religious beliefs in her personal and professional life.

10   _____. *Olga Korbut, Tears and Triumph*. St. Paul: EMC Corp., 40 pp.

Sketches the highlights in the career of the Russian gymnast, Olga Korbut. Describes her triumphs as a 1972 Olympic gold medalist and her subsequent drop to a second-place performer.

11   _____. *Shane Gould: Olympic Swimmer*. St. Paul: EMC Corp., 40 pp.

Offers a brief biography of Australian swimmer Shane Gould. Outlines the vigorous training and personal sacrifice which led to her winning five medals in the 1972 Olympic Games at the age of fifteen. Describes Gould's early family life; provides some insight into the joys and the difficulties of being in the public spotlight at such a young age.

12   JENSEN, MARLENE. *Improve Your Figure Through Sports*. Chatsworth, Calif.: Books for Better Living, 166 pp.

Makes a case for participation in sports as a means to a healthy, attractive figure rather than health spas and exercise routines. Comments about several sports to "start out with" such as swimming, bowling, badminton, volleyball, and golf and sports that provide vigorous activity to "work up to" such as tennis, skiing, racquetball, scuba diving, and hang gliding. Offers a positive rationale for sports rather than exercises for improving the figure.

13   KING, BILLIE JEAN, and HYAMS, JOE. *Billie Jean King's Secrets of Winning Tennis.* New York: Holt, Rinehart, & Winston, 126 pp.

Analyzes all elements of tennis needed to achieve success as a player. Is generally "female oriented," though instructional information may be used equally as well by men. Uses a format of questions about the various topics and King's answers to them. Includes a chapter on "Female Questions" composed of a variety of questions asked about women's tennis.

14   MAY, JULIAN. *Billie Jean King: Tennis Champion.* Mankato, Minn.: Crestwood House, 48 pp.

Describes King's childhood introduction to tennis, progresses chronologically through her career, and concludes with her famous match against Bobby Riggs in 1973.

15   McGINNIS, VERA. *Rodeo Road: My Life as a Pioneer Cowgirl.* New York: Hastings House, 225 pp.

Chronicles the riding career of McGinnis, one of the pioneers of women's rodeo, from her first stunt at the age of three to the abrupt conclusion of her rodeo riding in 1934 at thirty-nine, the result of a serious fall from her horse. Colorful descriptions of the world of rodeo are sprinkled with personal anecdotes from the rodeo circuit in the United States as well as exhibition riding in the Orient and the British Isles. Generously illustrated with photographs, which, with the text, provide a general history of women in the rodeo.

16   MILLER, DONNA MAE. *Coaching the Female Athlete.* Philadelphia: Lea and Febiger, 212 pp.

Contains a broad, theoretical analysis of coaching the female athlete with no attempt to include the coaching needs of specific sports. Discusses motor learning concepts, mechanical principles, training and conditioning procedures, and motivation techniques applicable to all sports. Provides a synthesis of the limited research conducted on the female athlete, particularly in the physiological and psychological areas.

17 MILLER, KENNETH D., and JONES, BILLIE J. *Track and Field for Girls*. New York: Ronald Press Co., 165 pp.
    Presents a brief summary of the history of track and field for women, primarily in relation to the modern Olympic Games; highlights the historical development of individual events. Includes performance techniques for all major events, information for planning a meet, and suggestions for coaching.

18 MORSE, CHARLES, and MORSE, ANN. *Evonne Goolagong*. Mankato, Minn.: Creative Education, 31 pp.
    Focuses on the early life of tennis champion Evonne Goolagong; describes the major events leading to her championship at Wimbledon in 1971.

19 _____. *Peggy Fleming*. Mankato, Minn.: Creative Education, 31 pp.
    Sketches the major events in Fleming's figure skating career leading to her gold-medal performance in the 1968 Olympic Games.

20 OLSEN, JAMES T. *Billie Jean King: The Lady of the Court*. Mankato, Minn.: Creative Education, 31 pp.
    Describes King's tennis career as a successful amateur and her work in trying to change the sport, particularly for women. Highlights her major tennis championships and some of the important incidents in her personal life.

21 ROBERTSON, MAX, ed. *The Encyclopedia of Tennis*. New York: Viking Press, 392 pp.
    Presents encyclopedic coverage of tennis; includes several women. Provides brief biographical data for many well-known players ranging from Maud Watson, the first Wimbledon champion, to Chris Evert and Evonne Goolagong of more recent fame. More detailed biographies for some women are found in a section titled "Great Players of All Time." "Centre Court Classics" describes five women's matches at Wimbledon considered to be among the best in tennis

history, and "The Women's Pro Game" outlines the development of women's professional tennis. A section on fashion provides a colorful history of women's tennis costumes, and a records section lists the winners of major tennis tournaments.

22   ROONEY, JOHN F. "Women's Sport." In *A Geography of American Sport*. Reading, Mass.: Addison-Wesley Publishing Co., pp. 242-253.

Provides data on the sports played by women and the amount of participation among women in the United States. Includes statistics for both high schools and colleges.

23   RUNNER'S WORLD MAGAZINE. *The Female Runner*. Mountain View, Calif.: World Publications, 31 pp.

Presents a compilation of articles concerned with the female runner. Considers the future of women's running, physiological aspects of training related to women, and psychological dimensions of the woman who chooses to be an athlete. Attempts to dispel the myths about the female athlete.

24   SLOANE, GLORIA, and COE, PHYLLIS. *How to Be a First-Rate First Mate*. New York: Quadrangle/The New York Times Book Co., 156 pp.

Serves as a practical guide for the novice sailor to help make boating a happy experience. Includes safety, planning cruises, equipping the galley, entertaining guests, sailing with children, rules of the "road," handling the boat on the water, and care of the boat on the return. Some readers may be displeased with subtle nuances that infer a second-class position for the woman sailor.

25   SMITH, JAY H. *Olga Korbut*. Mankato, Minn.: Creative Education, 31 pp.

Highlights the important events in the life and brief career of Russian gymnast Olga Korbut. Provides an overview of her life as a champion gymnast.

26   SPIRDUSO, WANEEN WYRICK, ed. *Bibliography of Research Involving Female Subjects*. Washington, D.C.: American Alliance for Health, Physical Education, and Recreation, 224 pp.

Includes titles of theses and dissertations from ninety-three institutions in which women were the subjects of the study. Provides author, title, year, and institution for the studies, which are organized under the following categories: motor learning; sport psychology; physiological aspects of motor performance; sport studies; physical education for the handicapped; health; teaching methods, curriculum, and administration; and recreation and leisure.

27 SULLIVAN, GEORGE. *Queens of the Court*. New York: Dodd, Mead & Co., 111 pp.

Provides résumés of the careers of six well-known tennis stars, Margaret Court, Rosemary Casals, Billie Jean King, Chris Evert, Evonne Goolagong, and Virginia Wade. Comments briefly on the important contributions to the development of tennis made by leading women players in the early developing years of the sport.

28 THIGPEN, JANET. *Power Volleyball for Girls and Women*. Dubuque, Iowa: William C. Brown Co., 144 pp.

Presents the sport of volleyball as it applies to girls and women, but much of the information is applicable to any player. Analyzes offensive and defensive skills and strategies; includes teaching progressions, a typical coaching session, and the psychology of coaching. Lists results of major tournaments for both women and men.

1975

1 ABBINANTI, DOROTHY; CARLSON, JOYCE; KAPSALIS, MARY; and KLINGER, ANNE. *Officiating Women's Sports*. Champaign, Ill.: Stipes Publishing Co., 109 pp.

Describes responsibilities and skills for officials in basketball, field hockey, softball, and volleyball. Clarifies differences in officiating techniques in volleyball and basketball among the governing bodies for the sports—United States Volleyball Association, National Association for Girls and Women's Sports, Amateur Athletic Union, and the National Federation.

2 BENNETT, BRUCE; HOWELL, MAXWELL L.; and SIMRI, URIEL. "Sport for Girls and Women." In *Comparative Physical Education and Sport*. Philadelphia: Lea and Febiger, pp. 175-187.

Discusses the emergence of the modern female athlete as a phenomenon of the twentieth century. Compares briefly the development of sport in various countries and identifies the United States as fulfilling a pioneer role in the development of women's sport as a result of Title IX of the Educational Amendments Act in 1972.

3   BURCHARD, MARSHALL, and BURCHARD, SUE H. *Sports Hero, Billie Jean King*. New York: G.P. Putnam's Sons, 95 pp.
   Relates the story of Billie Jean King's tennis career beginning with her learning to play the game on the public courts of Long Beach, California. Describes her first Wimbledon championship, her rise to the number one ranking, her move to the professional circuit, and her much publicized match with Bobby Riggs. Includes some of her efforts to upgrade the sport of tennis, particularly in the professional realm.

4   CHARLES, ALLEGRA. *How to Win at Ladies Doubles*. New York: Arco Publishing Co., 151 pp.
   Briefly outlines the basics of doubles play, but perhaps misleading to the reader who expects a thorough analysis of the doubles game. Includes several chapters on basic fundamentals of tennis; discusses such diverse topics as tennis rackets, court surfaces, tennis elbow, and tennis and sex.

5   CONROY, MARY. *The Rational Woman's Guide to Self Defense*. New York: Grosset & Dunlap, 128 pp.
   Begins with basic self-defense strategies and a long list of suggestions for avoiding confrontation. Describes and illustrates basic techniques of kicking, striking, and releases from assailants' holds; presents suggestions for using simple weapons and precautions necessary in their use. Discusses rape and what to do in case of such assault, emphasizing reporting the crime and follow-up procedures.

6   COURT, MARGARET SMITH, and McGANN, GEORGE. *Court on Court: A Life of Tennis*. New York: Dodd, Mead & Co., 211 pp.
   Describes Court's introduction to tennis as a young child in Australia, her early touring and success as an amateur, and her induction into professional tennis. Includes a discussion about her concern for the demise of good sportsmanship and the loss of the amateur spirit in tennis as money becomes an increasingly important

factor in the professional game. Court is candid in her admiration for the skill of many of her competitors, but critical of players when she believes "big money" has made a change in attitude and relationships with others.

7   ELDRED, PATRICIA MULROONEY. *Kathy Whitworth*. Mankato, Minn.: Creative Education, 31 pp.
       Briefly details the professional career of golfer Kathy Whitworth.

8   GEMME, LEILA B. *The New Breed of Athlete*. New York: Pocket Books, 190 pp.
       Focuses on athletes who differed in some way from the usual, those who shook the sports establishment. Includes information on Kathy Kusner (pp. 79-91), the first woman licensed to race on the flat track or in major legalized gambling races, and Billie Jean King (pp. 120-136), outspoken advocate for equality in women's sports.

9   GLEASNER, DIANA D. *Women in Sports: Swimming*. New York: Harvey House, 63 pp.
       Provides a cursory review of the history of swimming; presents brief highlights in the aquatic careers of diver Christine Loock; speed swimmers Shirley Babashoff and Kathy Heddy; synchronized swimmer Gail Buzonas; and marathon swimmer Diana Nyad.

10   GOOLAGONG, EVONNE, and COLLINS, BUD. *Evonne! On the Move*. New York: E.P. Dutton & Co., 190 pp.
       Presents a personal account of Goolagong's introduction to the sport of tennis, her rise to the top as a competitor, and ultimately, her move into the professional ranks. The book is sprinkled with anecdotes about life with her family, her coach and mentor, Vic Edwards, and her travels on the tennis circuit. Provides an overview of one woman's rise to tennis fame, in this case, an unusual accomplishment considering her background as an aborigine from the Australian outback.

11   HANEY, LYNN. *Ride 'em Cowgirl!* New York: G.P. Putnam's Sons, 128 pp.

Uses the colorful terminology of the rodeo to convey the atmosphere of the rodeo world in which wo men participate. Explains the structure of professional rodeo, including the seven events of all-girl rodeos under the aegis of the Girls' Rodeo Association, and the two events, barrel racing and team roping, of the Rodeo Cowboys' Association which women may enter.

12 HAYNIE, SANDRA. *Golf: A Natural Course for Women*. New York: Atheneum, 208 pp.

Based on the belief that all women have the timing, body control, and natural grace to learn golf and enjoy it. Provides suggestions for conditioning, tips on perfecting and improving performance, selecting appropriate equipment, and ideas about how to look, what to wear, and how to act on the course. Takes a somewhat different and refreshing approach from the usual instructional manual.

13 JACOBS, HELEN HULL. *Famous Modern American Women Athletes*. New York: Dodd, Mead & Co., 136 pp.

Provides brief biographies of eight American women who have achieved success in their different sports. Career highlights are included for Judy Cook Soutar, bowling; Janet Lynn, figure skating; Micki King, diving; Kathy Whitworth, golf; Cindy Nelson, skiing; Shirley Babashoff, swimming; Billie Jean King, tennis; and Francie Larrieu, track.

14 JACOBS, LINDA. *Annemarie Proell: Queen of the Mountain*. St. Paul: EMC Corp., 40 pp.

Briefly outlines the career of Annemarie Proell, the Austrian skier who had won thirty-one individual races, a record unmatched by any other skier, male or female. A major focus is on Proell's attitude toward winning and losing and the ways in which she handles that aspect of competition.

15 ____. *Cathy Rigby: On the Beam*. St. Paul: EMC Corp., 40 pp.

Briefly sketches the life and career of gymnast Cathy Rigby, the first American to win a medal in international competition at the World Gymnastics Championships in Yugoslavia in 1970.

16 ____. *Evonne Goolagong: Smiles and Smashes*. St. Paul: EMC Corp., 40 pp.

Describes Goolagong's 1971 Wimbledon championship, then backtracks to the beginning of her tennis career in Barellan, Australia. Discusses the influence of her coach, Victor Edwards, in her rise to successful amateur and professional play. Offers some insight into Goolagong's personal feelings about herself as a well-known tennis personality.

17 ____. *Joan Moore Rice: The Olympic Dream*. St. Paul: EMC Corp., 40 pp.

Briefly describes the gymnastics career of Olympic competitor Joan Moore Rice, who gave up her dreams of participation in the 1976 Games to become a teacher of future Olympians. Highlights her early introduction to gymnastics and her major successes in competition. Generously illustrated with photographs.

18 ____. *Laura Baugh: Golf's Golden Girl*. St. Paul: EMC Corp., 40 pp.

Briefly sketches Laura Baugh's golf career from her first attempts with a handmade club at the age of four to her joining the professional ranks at eighteen. Describes Baugh's early personal life and some of her interests other than golf.

19 ____. *Mary Decker: Speed Records and Spaghetti*. St. Paul: EMC Corp., 40 pp.

Relates the highlights in the brief track career of Mary Decker, who broke world speed records at the age of fifteen. Presents glimpses of her personal life along with anecdotes of some of the unusual occurrences in her competitions.

20 ____. *Rosemary Casals: The Rebel Rosebud*. St. Paul: EMC Corp., 40 pp.

Briefly outlines Casal's tennis career, focusing primarily on her experiences as a professional player. Describes her beginning interest in tennis and some of the incidents that contributed to her being called a rebel among the tennis set.

21 ____. *Wilma Rudolph: Run for Glory*. St. Paul: EMC Corp., 40 pp.

Sketches the life and running career of Wilma Rudolph, first woman to win three gold medals in track in a single Olympics competition. Describes her early struggle with polio and her career as a track scholarship athlete at Tennessee State University. Concludes with a brief section on her life as a wife, mother, and career woman.

22   JOYCE, JOAN, and ANQUILLAN, JOHN. *Winning Softball*. Chicago: Henry Regnery Co., 109 pp.

Designed for use by both women and men; analyzes the basic skills of pitching, batting, and fielding; includes conditioning techniques for players. Compares the women's and men's games; clarifies the differences between the fast-pitch game and the slow-pitch game.

23   KING, BILLIE JEAN, with CHAPIN, KIM. *Billie Jean*. London: W. H. Allen, 208 pp.

Presents a detailed analysis of King's tennis career. Includes her growing up years in Long Beach, California, her budding interest in tennis, and her successes and failures as an amateur. A good portion of the book is devoted to her career in professional tennis and her crusade for equity for women players. Contains a candid discussion of her abortion and the unpleasant publicity associated with it. Describes her highly publicized match with Bobby Riggs.

24   LARDNER, REX. *Tactics in Women's Singles, Doubles, and Mixed Doubles*. Garden City, N.Y.: Doubleday & Co., 135 pp.

Devoted primarily to simple strategies, both offensive and defensive. Reviews basic tennis strokes; includes a list of definitions of tennis terms.

25   MACKSEY, JOAN, and MACKSEY, KENNETH M. *The Book of Women's Achievements*. New York: Stein and Day, 288 pp.

Covers diverse accomplishments of women from artists to wartime endeavors. Includes brief biographical data and their major sporting achievements for fifty-five sportswomen.

26   MAY, JULIAN. *Chris Evert: Princess of Tennis*. Mankato, Minn.: Crestwood House, 48 pp.

Provides a brief narrative of Evert's tennis career from her first lessons to her participation in professional tennis. Generously illustrated with photographs of Evert in action.

27   . *Janet Lynn: Figure Skating Star*. Mankato, Minn.: Crestwood House, 48 pp.
Sketches the highlights of Janet Lynn's amateur skating career. Describes her introduction and early successes as well as her failure to win the coveted gold medal in either the Olympic Games in 1972 or the World Championships in 1973.

28   . *Wimbledon World Tennis Focus*. Mankato, Minn.: Creative Education, 47 pp.
Provides a brief history of the tennis tournament at Wimbledon; includes biographical sketches of women singles champions Gussie Moran, Margaret Court, Evonne Goolagong, Billie Jean King, and Chris Evert and mentions several others. Includes a complete list of singles champions at Wimbledon, both women and men, through 1974.

29   MAYO, JANE, with GRAY, BOB. *Championship Barrel Racing*. Houston: Cordovan Corp., 85 pp.
Summarizes the history of the sport of barrel racing; describes the important aspects of selecting and training the barrel horse. Provides a progressive analysis of the skills and techniques needed to become a successful barrel racer.

30   MEADE, MARION. *Women in Sports: Tennis* New York: Harvey House, 78 pp.
Describes major events in the rise to stardom of top-ranked players Billie Jean King, Rosemary Casals, Chris Evert, Evonne Goolagong Cawley, and Margaret Court. Notes the problems encountered by women in attempting to achieve the financial success which was later possible in women's professional tennis.

31   MORSE, ANN. *Janet Lynn*. Mankato, Minn.: Creative Education, 31 pp.

Briefly describes the high points of Lynn's successful skating career in 1973. Focuses on the successes and failures of a young woman who won several skating medals yet seemed to lack the strong desire to win.

32 NEAL, PATSY, and TUTKO, THOMAS A. *Coaching Girls and Women, Psychological Perspectives*. Boston: Allyn & Bacon, 235 pp.

Provides unusual insight into the coaching of female athletes. Rather than offering the practical "how to" kinds of information for coaches, the authors have delved into the processes for understanding the woman coach and woman athlete. Provocative chapter titles entice one to read further in the section on understanding the athlete: "Hassles and Hang-ups," "The Achievement-Oriented Female in American Society," "Why Play?" and "The Female Athlete in the Emotional Milieu of Sport." Final chapters offer practical advice for coaches, and excellent bibliographies are included throughout the book.

33 PIRNAT, JANET WENGER. *Personal Defence Skills for Women*. Champaign, Ill.: Stipes Publishing Co., 111 pp.

Designed as a text for either the self-learner or in a teacher-directed class. Covers personal defense skills for a variety of different types of physical attack. Presents units of basic and advanced defensive skills, structured in ten progressive lessons. Analyzes skills, describes common errors, presents evaluation techniques. Illustrated with photographs for each skill presented.

34 RESICK, MATTHEW C., and ERICKSON, CARL E. *Intercollegiate and Interscholastic Athletics for Men and Women*. Reading, Mass.: Addison-Wesley, 285 pp.

Focuses on administrative procedures for athletics programs, both high school and college, including financing, facilities, eligibility and recruitment, and public relations. Includes a section specifically concerned with the development of athletic programs for girls and women.

35 RYAN, JOAN. *Contributions of Women: Sports*. Minneapolis: Dillon Press, 136 pp.

Features biographies of six successful female athletes. Brief sketches present career highlights for Babe Didrikson Zaharias, all-around sportswoman; Kathy Kusner, Olympic equestrienne; Wilma Rudolph, Olympic runner; Billie Jean King, tennis star; Peggy Fleming, Olympic figure skater; and Melissa Belote, young swimming champion. A final section is devoted to brief comments on the athletic careers of eight other women: Gertrude Ederle, Althea Gibson, Sonja Henie, Micki King, Helen Wills Moody, Cathy Rigby, Eleonora Sears, and Wyomia Tyus.

36 SABIN, FRANCENE. *Women Who Win*. New York: Random House, 185 pp.

Presents brief biographies of fourteen women champion athletes. Emphasizes the athletic achievements of women in the 1960s and 1970s who have helped prepare the way for others to attain success. Includes sketches for Billie Jean King; Janet Lynn; Cheryl Toussaint; Paula Sperber; Cathy Rigby; Micki King; Kathy Whitworth; Marilyn, Barbara, and Lindy Cochran; and Jenny Bartz, Lynn Genesko, Nina MacInnis, and Sharon Berg, the first American women to receive nationally recognized collegiate swimming scholarships.

37 SAUNDERS, VIVIEN. *The Complete Woman Golfer*. London: Stanley Paul & Co., 202 pp.

Written for beginning golfers, using nontechnical language to analyze golf skills and suggest strategies for difficult strokes. Includes advice for selecting equipment; concludes with a detailed glossary of golf terms.

38 SHANE, GEORGE. *Sportraits of the Stars*. Toronto: Gall Publications, 111 pp.

Relates the achievement records of several athletes, both women and men, with a brief biography illustrated with a caricature drawing. Women included are Janet Lynn, Shane Gould, Margaret Court, Annemarie Proell, Marlene Stewart Streit, Violetta Nesvkaitis, Olga Korbut, Karen Magnussen, Billie Jean King, and Sylvia Burka.

39 SMITH, JAY H. *Chris Evert*. Mankato, Minn.: Creative Education Society, 31 pp.

Presents brief highlights in Evert's tennis career, including her first Wimbledon championship in 1974.

40 STAMBLER, IRWIN. *Women in Sports*. Garden City, N.Y.: Doubleday & Co., 155 pp.

Offers a brief overview of the struggle women have had in achieving sports opportunities; reviews the individual accomplishments of sportswomen in several different fields of endeavor. Included are Cathy Rigby, Billie Jean King, Anne Henning, Robyn Smith, Wyomia Tyus, Mary Decker, Babe Didrikson Zaharias, Melissa Belote, Shirley Muldowney, Barbara Ann Cochran, Micki King, and Theresa Shank.

41 SUPONEV, MICHAEL. *Olga Korbut: A Biographical Portrait*. Garden City, N.Y.: Doubleday & Co., 87 pp.

Presents biographical information about Soviet gymnast Olga Korbut; stresses her career, the training and development of a champion, and the daily routine required to succeed as an Olympic competitor.

42 VALENS, E.G. *The Other Side of the Mountain*. New York: Warner Books, 285 pp.

Presents the story of skier Jill Kinmont, an aspiring Olympic contender, whose career ended with a serious skiing accident that left her paralyzed from the shoulders down. Focuses on her life just prior to the accident and her uphill climb through therapy to become a successful teacher.

Chapter 4

Women's Sport Comes of Age, 1976-1990

As the nation celebrated its bicentennial and moved into the last quarter of the twentieth century, the future of women in many realms appeared remarkably bright. Growing numbers of women were moving into the traditional male professions as the doors of law, medicine, engineering, and the ministry opened wider for them. Barriers were lowered in such sex-segregated occupations as firefighting, policing, and bartending. Sally Ride became the first female crew member in space, and Geraldine Ferraro ran for vice president.

Discrimination against women has nonetheless persisted, evident in wages, in the kinds of jobs generally available, and in efforts to reach the top of the corporate ladder. Few top executives are women; the labor force, for the most part, is still sex-segregated; and women's earnings fall far short of those of men's. The Civil Rights Restoration Act has offered new hope for equity, and women, themselves, have continued to work diligently toward equality in all phases of their lives.

Opportunities for the growing numbers of avid sports enthusiasts have reached extraordinary heights. Although Title IX may not have fulfilled its potential in many areas, progress in the sporting arena is obvious. Interscholastic and intercollegiate programs for women are well established across the nation, and a financially supported education is now available to the highly skilled woman, as it has been to men for decades. Athletic growth beyond college years is still limited for women in many sports for lack of professional opportunities so readily available to men. Women's professional basketball, softball, and volleyball have achieved only limited success. In the individual sports of bowling, tennis, and golf, however, women's horizons have broadened, perhaps because these are still more acceptable to a society that has traditionally viewed team sports in particular as a masculine endeavor. At long last the myths about women's capabilities in sport and about the physiological destruction caused by strenuous activity are being put to rest. Women *can* run the marathon, as was so ably evidenced by Joan Benoit when the Women's Marathon was finally added to the 1984 Olympics program. All-women's teams have scaled some of the world's highest mountains, and Susan Butcher captured a third win in the grueling 1100 mile Iditarod Trail dogsled race in Alaska. Research on women involved in physical activities of all kinds has increased, but it remains far behind that using male subjects.

The achievements of outstanding sportswomen are numerous and are reported regularly in the sports section of the newspaper rather than in the women's section. Young girls now have their own heroes, athletes of their own sex to emulate. Of greatest importance, however, is the increasing number of girls and women who participate in sport for personal rewards and pleasure. Whether old, young, skilled, disabled, pregnant, or physically fit, women may be found in a seemingly limitless array of sporting activities.

1976

1   BROWN, FERN G. *Racing Against the Odds: Robyn G. Smith*. Milwaukee: Raintree Editions, 47 pp.
       Relates the events in Robyn Smith's struggle to become a jockey, even though she had never ridden a horse. Describes her experiences in learning to ride, her first races, her later successes, and her continued efforts to be accepted in the racing world.

2   BURCHARD, SUE H. *Chris Evert*. New York: Harcourt Brace Jovanovich, 64 pp.
       Highlights the tennis career of Chris Evert, including her amateur successes and her professional endeavors. Provides brief glimpses into her personal life.

3   BUTCHER, GRACE. *Women in Sports: Motorcycling*. New York: Harvey House, 63 pp.
       Devoted primarily to competitive motorcycle racing. Gives a brief introduction to the special equipment used in the sport and the

techniques of learning to ride. Includes the exploits of eight women racers, their entry into and involvement with motorcycling.

4   DARDEN, ANNE. *The Sports Hall of Fame*. New York: Drake Publishers, 236 pp.

Includes brief biographical information and photographs of fourteen sportswomen, primarily athletes from the past three decades. Does highlight the careers of Sonja Henie, Helen Wills, and Babe Didrikson from the earlier period.

5   DONOVAN, HEDLEY, ed. *Remarkable American Women, 1776-1976*. New York: Time, 116 pp.

Includes several athletes selected "either because of the notable things they have done or the extraordinary lives they have led" (p. 2). Brief paragraphs, accompanied by photographs, note the accomplishments of Tenley Albright, Gertrude Ederle, Billie Jean King, Andrea Mead Lawrence, Wilma Rudolph, Eleonora Sears, Helen Wills, and Babe Didrikson Zaharias.

6   DUNKLE, MARGARET. *Competitive Athletics: In Search of Equal Opportunity*. Washington, D.C.: U.S. Department of Health, Education, and Welfare, 142 pp.

Designed to provide technical assistance to agencies and institutions to ensure compliance with Title IX of the Educational Amendments Act of 1972. Prepared primarily by athletic directors, administrators, and coaches to eliminate sex discrimination in athletic programs. General information concerning equal opportunity in athletic programs is followed by chapters on specific aspects of compliance with Title IX. Model assessment tools are provided for use in evaluating each of the several areas of concern. A bibliography of selected resources concerned with equity concludes the manual.

7   ELLIOT, LEN, and KELLY, BARBARA. *Who's Who in Golf*. New Rochelle, N.Y.: Arlington House Publishers, 208 pp.

Includes brief biographical data and the major golf championships of the top women golfers from as early as 1896. Criteria for selecting women players for the book, which also includes men, were: amateurs with two or more Curtis Cup team memberships or one World Cup team membership, professionals who had won at least once on the LPGA tour, or All Americans who had won a national championship, amateur or professional.

8 ENRIGHT, JIM. *Only in Iowa*. Des Moines: Iowa Girls' High School Athletic Union, 324 pp.

Details the historical development of girls' interscholastic basketball in Iowa, beginning with the establishment of the Girls' High School Athletic Union in 1926. Describes some of the personalities, both coaches and players, involved with the sport; provides a long list of statistics for basketball and other girls' high school sports. Discusses the Girls' Hall of Fame established in 1961.

9 GAULT, JIM, with GRANT, JACK. *The World of Women's Gymnastics*. Millbrae, Calif.: Celestial Arts, 141 pp.

Explores the many facets of the sport of gymnastics outside the realm of skill analysis. Considers the mental and emotional attitudes necessary for success, the influence of parents in gymnastics training, the problems and pitfalls of the international gymnastics judge, and some of the political aspects evident in the 1976 Olympic Games.

10 GEMME, LEILA BOYLE. *King on the Court: Billie Jean King*. Milwaukee: Raintree Editions, 47 pp.

Describes King's introduction to and progress in amateur tennis and her major championship successes. Relates her efforts to change tennis from a sport for the wealthy only to one for the "average guy" and her often criticized work as a professional player attempting to gain equity for women in the sport.

11 GUNDLING, BEULAH. *Dancing in the Water*. Cedar Rapids, Iowa: Beulah Gundling, 261 pp.

Presents an autobiography of synchronized swimmer Beulah Gundling. Details her competitive and exhibition swimming and her interest in choreography. Generously illustrated with photographs.

12 HANEY, LYNN. *Chris Evert, the Young Champion*. New York: G.P. Putnam's Sons, 127 pp.

Focuses primarily on Evert's professional career with brief sketches of her early years in tennis and her amateur successes.

Describes her major professional experiences, including significant information about several of her competitors. Julie Anthony, Evonne Goolagong, Martina Navratilova, and Billie Jean King all receive more than cursory mention by the author.

13   HAUSER, HILLARY. *Women in Sports: Scuba Diving.* New York: Harvey House, 79 pp.

Includes brief sketches of highlights in the lives of five women involved in underwater careers. Each of the five, Valerie Taylor, Eugenie Clark, Kati Garner, Zale Parry, and Sylvia Earle, is representative of the diverse occupations from U. S. Navy diver to underwater actress which are available to women.

14   HERDA, D.J. *Free Spirit: Evonne Goolagong.* Milwaukee: Raintree Editions, 47 pp.

Traces Goolagong's rise from "ball girl" at the age of five to Wimbledon champion at nineteen. Describes her major championships and her activities after joining the professional circuit.

15   HOLLANDER, PHYLLIS. *100 Greatest Women in Sports.* New York: Grosset & Dunlap, 142 pp.

Provides brief sketches of the exploits of more than 100 women athletes in eighteen different sports with photographs of almost all of them. Highlights the outstanding accomplishments of pioneers in the sports world in the early 1900s as well as modern champions. Reviews women's successes as athletes since the turn of the century, not only in sports which have long been the domain of the female, tennis, figure skating, and swimming, but also in areas more recently invaded by women, marathon running and horse racing.

16   HUEY, LYNDA. *A Running Start.* New York: Quadrangle/New York Times Book Co., 254 pp.

Portrays the world of the female athlete, with the pleasures it offers and the struggles necessary to achieve success in it. Vividly details Huey's experiences as a track athlete and her involvement with some of the more dramatic sports events in recent years. Discusses her relationships with athletes at San Jose State who were later involved in the Olympic Boycott Movement in 1968, her teaching stint at Oberlin College, and her participation with Wilt's Wonder Women, a track club sponsored by Wilt Chamberlain. Emphasizes the real joy found in sports participation, the problems women face in becoming successful athletes, and the strong pressures on women to conform to the female norm.

17   JACOBS, LINDA. *Cindy Nelson: North Country Skier*. St. Paul: EMC Corp., 40 pp.
       Presents a brief biographical sketch of Cindy Nelson, downhill skier, who won the World Cup title after recovering from a serious injury. Describes her early life in Lutsen, Minnesota, where she learned to ski and developed into a champion at her parents' ski resort.

18   _____. *Madeline Manning Jackson: Running on Faith*. St. Paul: EMC Corp., 39 pp.
       Provides a brief account of highlights in the life of runner Madeline Jackson. Emphasizes her religious devotion and its effect on her life.

19   _____. *Martina Navratilova: Tennis Fury*. St. Paul: EMC Corp., 40 pp.
       Describes Navratilova's early years in Czechoslovakia and her parents' efforts to steer her into a sport for girls. Relates her successes as a tennis champion, the problems with government control of her career, and her decision to seek asylum in the United States in 1975.

20   _____. *Robin Campbell: Joy in the Morning*. St. Paul: EMC Corp., 40 pp.
       Focuses on Campbell's personal life; describes her introduction to running and the successes that made her a possible contender in the 1980 Olympic Games.

21   _____. *Robyn Smith: In Silks*. St. Paul: EMC Corp., 40 pp.
       Details Smith's efforts to become a jockey and her early experiences in the racing world after giving up the idea of an acting career. Describes her experiences in New York as a reasonably successful jockey, one of the very few women in the profession.

22   KNEER, MARIAN E., and McCORD, CHARLES L. *Softball: Slow and Fast Pitch*. Dubuque, Iowa: William C. Brown Co., 96 pp.

Departs from the usual format for instructional manuals. Chapters begin with instructional objectives which identify the content that follows; intersperses self-evaluation questions throughout the book to help determine attainment of stated objectives. Includes offensive and defensive skills, patterns of play, language and lore of the game, rules, selection and care of equipment, conditioning, and suggestions for teacher and coach.

23   MAY, JULIAN. *Forest Hills and the American Tennis Championship*. Mankato, Minn.: Creative Educational Society, 47 pp.

Sketches the highlights in the tennis careers of several Forest Hills champions, both women and men. Contains information about Molla Bjurstedt Mallory, Suzanne Lenglen, Helen Wills, Helen Hull Jacobs, Alice Marble, Maureen Connolly, Althea Gibson, Billie Jean King, and Chris Evert. A list of champions at Forest Hills through 1975 is included.

24   MICHENER, JAMES A. "Women in Sports." In *Sports in America*. New York: Random House, pp. 120-143.

Briefly examines the role of women in sport, focusing on four questions: Are girls so biologically different from men that sports are injurious to them? Should girls and boys play on the same teams? What new legal developments affect this problem? and In state-supported institutions, what would be a reasonable allocation of public funds for women's sports and for men's? (p. 122).

25   MILLER, LUREE. *On Top of the World: Five Women Explorers in Tibet*. New York: Paddington Press.

Profiles five of the women who climbed in the high Himalayas between 1850 and 1920; includes brief biographical data.

26   MORSE, ANN. *Tennis Champion, Billie Jean King*. Mankato, Minn.: Creative Educational Society, 31 pp.

Focuses on King's life with brief comments about her tennis career.

27 NOVAK, MICHAEL. "Of Women and Sports." In *The Joy of Sports*. New York: Basic Books Publishers, pp. 191-204.

Focuses primarily on cultural mores and the relationship of these to women's involvement with sport.

28 O'SHEA, MARY JO. *Laura Baugh*. Mankato, Minn.: Creative Education, 31 pp.

Details the golf career of Laura Baugh; emphasizes her early life and the experience that shaped her athletic success. Final pages describe her professional career that began at the age of eighteen.

29 PAISH, WILF, and DUFFY, TONY. *Athletics in Focus*. London: Lepus Books, 163 pp.

Captures the essence of track and field athletics through the eye of the camera. Narrative information is minimal; about half of the ninety-two illustrations are photographs of women.

30 READ, BRENDA. *Better Hockey for Girls*. London: Kaye & Ward, 95 pp.

Describes skills and techniques for developing successful play in field hockey.

31 READ, BRENDA, and WALKER, FREDA. *Advanced Hockey for Women*. London: Faber & Faber, 166 pp.

Focuses on material of specific interest to advanced players. Includes information on performing advanced skills, assessing opponents' play, tactical possibilities from set plays, and plays usable in unorthodox situations.

32 RUSH, CATHY, and MIFFLIN, LOWRIE. *Women's Basketball*. New York: Hawthorn Books, 132 pp.

Written for the person interested in learning the game of basketball. Utilizes the technique of talking to the reader in describing the components that develop a strong player – attitude, conditioning, basic skills, and offensive and defensive tactics.

33 RYAN, FRANK. *Gymnastics for Girls*. New York: Viking Press, 431 pp.

Offers a comprehensive view of gymnastics for women. Provides skill analysis, teaching techniques, skill progressions, and corrections for common errors for each event. Examines the coaching role, offering special advice for the person in that position. Covers basic and advanced skill levels; is well illustrated with photographs and drawings.

34 SCHMID, ANDREA B. *Modern Rhythmic Gymnastics*. Palo Alto, Calif.: Mayfield Publishing Co., 379 pp.

Offers a history of rhythmic gymnastics, clarifying the differences between this and other forms of gymnastics. Provides skill analysis for using balls, ropes, hoops, ribbons, clubs, scarves, flags, and wands. Describes basic dance movements and movement combinations with the hand apparatus for use with this form of gymnastics.

35 SMITH, BEATRICE S. *Babe: Mildred Didrikson Zaharias*. Milwaukee: Raintree Publications, 48 pp.

Outlines the sports career of Babe Zaharias. Describes her achievements in basketball, track, and golf and her return to championship status in golf after her first battle with cancer.

36 STEINER, BRADLEY J. *Below the Belt: Unarmed Combat for Women*. Boulder, Col.: Paladin Press, 168 pp.

Emphasizes physical fitness, speed, determination, ruthlessness, and surprise in dealing with personal attack. Includes physical defense techniques as well as the use of weapons for protection.

37 SUGANO, JUN. *Karate and Self-Defense for Women*. London: Ward Lock, 119 pp.

Analyzes basic fundamentals of karate; drawing from those skills, presents techniques of self-defense for a variety of possible dangerous situations. Suggests a series of calisthenics for developing flexibility and stamina as well as improving concentration and control of power as a basis for becoming more capable of self-protection.

38   THACHER, ALIDA M. *Raising a Racket: Rosemary Casals*. Milwaukee: Raintree Editions, 47 pp.

Outlines Casals's tennis career, focusing on her move to professional tennis and her attempts to improve the opportunities for women in that area.

39   ULLYOT, JOAN. *Women's Running*. Mountain View, Calif.: World Publications, 153 pp.

Offers detailed information to the woman interested in running either for health and fitness or for racing. Includes basic principles for selecting shoes and clothing, warm-up activities, and safety; examines physiological aspects of running and provides information related to women. Describes techniques for beginners, intermediates, and racers; makes a careful distinction between running for fitness and running in competition.

40   VAN STEENWYK, ELIZABETH. *Women in Sports: Figure Skating*. New York: Harvey House, 79 pp.

Presents a review of the historical development of figure skating and basic rules and elements of competition for the sport. Includes brief biographical sketches of five champion skaters, Peggy Fleming, Janet Lynn, Karen Magnussen, Dianne deLeeuw, and Dorothy Hamill.

41   VANNIER, MARYHELEN, and POINDEXTER, HALLY B.W. *Individual and Team Sports for Girls and Women*, 3d ed. 781 pp.

Includes information updated from the first (1960.4) and second (1968.7) editions representing changes in approaches to teaching and methodology. Reflects major rules changes in basketball. A special feature of the book continues to be the inclusion of suggested readings, audiovisual materials, and periodicals for each of the sports.

42   WARREN, WILLIAM E. *Team Patterns in Girls' and Women's Basketball*. New York: A.S. Barnes & Co., 240 pp.

Devoted entirely to offensive and defensive strategies for women's basketball. Is unique in that all material deals with the six-player game, rather than the five-player game, which is almost universally played by girls and women.

1977

1   ADRIAN, MARLENE, and BRAME, JUDY, eds. *NAGWS Research Reports*. vol. 3, Washington, D.C.: American Alliance for Health, Physical Education, and Recreation, 188 pp.
Reports on specific research projects using female athletes as subjects; other articles suggest techniques which may be appropriate for conducting research on female sports participants.

2   BEISSER, ARNOLD R. "On Being a Woman and an Athlete." In *The Madness in Sport*. Bowie, Md.: Charles Press Publishers, pp. 65-80.
Presents a case study of a promising young woman tennis player who suddenly disappeared from the sports scene and reappeared a decade later. Relates her psychological struggles with her femininity and society's acceptance of the female athlete.

3   BERG, PATTY, with SCHIEWE, MARSH. *Inside Golf for Women*. Chicago: Contemporary Books, 104 pp.
Offers a step-by-step analysis of the skills of golf with practice suggestions for improving one's game. Includes advice for some of the difficult situations encountered in the game such as playing out of sand traps and uphill or sidehill shots.

4   BLALOCK, JANE, and NETLAND, DWAYNE. *The Guts to Win*. New York: Simon & Schuster, 158 pp.
Chronicles the life and career of professional golfer Jane Blalock; details her lengthy conflict with the Ladies' Professional Golf Association when accused of cheating. The book is sprinkled throughout with helpful instructional techniques for improving one's golf game.

5   BURCHARD, SUE H. *Sports Star, Nadia Comaneci*. New York: Harcourt Brace Jovanovich, 64 pp.
Sketches the background that led Nadia Comaneci to her outstanding performance in the 1976 Olympic Games. Describes her early life and training to become a gymnast and her perfect score performances at Montreal.

6 CAMPBELL, GAIL. *Marathon: The World of the Long-Distance Athlete*. New York: Sterling Publishing Co., 176 pp.

Provides general information about distance running, swimming, and bicycling; highlights major accomplishments of individuals who have competed in the events. Includes swimmers Gertrude Ederle, Florence Chadwick, Greta Andersen, Lynn Cox, Diana Nyad, Marilyn Bell, and Marty Sinn. Remarks on the early efforts of Kathy Switzer and Roberta Bingay to enter the Boston Marathon.

7 DARDEN, ELLINGTON. *Especially for Women*. West Point, N.Y.: Leisure Press, 227 pp.

Contains a collection of articles on health and fitness written in nontechnical, easy-to-understand language. Includes topics on strength training for women, diet and nutrition, physical fitness, exercise and pregnancy, and strength training after age fifty.

8 DEATHERAGE, DOROTHY, and REID, C. PATRICIA. *Administration of Women's Competitive Sports*. Dubuque, Iowa: William C. Brown Co., 267 pp.

Includes the mechanical aspects of administering competitive sports programs such as policies and procedures, public relations, coaching, and organization. The authors have also considered the philosophic bases for the conduct of such programs for women. A section on the historical development of competitive sports for women is included, and a lengthy appendix provides samples of materials in current use for administrative purposes.

9 DOLAN, EDWARD F., Jr., and LYTTLE, RICHARD D. *Martina Navratilova*. Garden City, N.Y.: Doubleday & Co., 81 pp.

Outlines Navratilova's early life and tennis pursuits and her defection from Czechoslovakia to the United States in order to have freedom to pursue her career. Describes her major amateur successes and highlights of her play as a professional.

10 FOREMAN, KEN, and HUSTED, VIRGINIA. *Track and Field Techniques for Girls and Women*, 3d ed. Dubuque, Iowa: William C. Brown Co., 297 pp.

Originally published in 1965 (2), second edition in 1971 (4). Motor learning principles have been eliminated; skill analysis and performance techniques have been altered to reflect new research information. Includes training schedules actually used by a successful competitor.

11 FRANCIS, CLARE. *Come Hell or High Water.* London: Pelham Books, 198 pp.

Presents a personal account of the author's participation in the 1976 Singlehanded Transatlantic Race from Plymouth, England to Newport, Rhode Island. Details the problems of sailing in heavy seas, fog, and among icebergs to finish in thirteenth place in twenty-nine days. Provides insight into why sailors are willing to risk their lives on long ocean voyages in spite of the loneliness and rigors that must be endured.

12 ____. *Woman Alone.* New York: David McKay Co., 191 pp.

Is almost identical to *Come Hell or High Water*, also published in 1977 (11). Minor changes have been made in words or phrases, and some illustrative photographs are different.

13 GEADELMANN, PATRICIA; GRANT, CHRISTINE; SLATTON, YVONNE; and BURKE, N. PEGGY. *Equality in Sports for Women.* Washington, D.C.: American Alliance for Health, Physical Education, and Recreation, 202 pp.

Designed as a manual to provide the tools for eliminating sex-biased discrimination and inequality in sports. A broad range of information is covered and includes the following: clarification of federal regulations relating to equity; ways and places to file a complaint if inequity is believed to exist; nationally organized women's groups and civil rights and professional groups whose work focuses on equality of opportunity; a summary of fifteen court cases on sex discrimination in athletics; and procedures for effecting change when inequities exist. A detailed appendix of basic information for dealing with inequities and a long list of references further enhance this collection of tools for effecting change in sports programs.

14 GLEASNER, DIANA C. *Women in Sports: Track and Field.* New York: Harvey House Publishers, 77 pp.

Provides a brief history of track and field for women; includes brief biographical sketches of runners Thelma Wright and Robin Campbell; hurdler Patty van Wolvelaere; high jumper Joni Huntley; javelin thrower Kathy Schmidt; and pentathlete Jane Frederick.

15 GRUMEZA, IAN. *Nadia*. New York: Hawthorn Books, 127 pp.
Chronicles the life and brief career of champion gymnast Nadia Comaneci; describes the qualities that made her successful, the rigorous schedule that is part of being a champion, and some of the competitions in which she astounded audiences with her record-breaking performances.

16 GUTMAN, BILL. *Modern Women Superstars*. New York: Dodd, Mead & Co., 112 pp.
Briefly sketches the sports careers of six women athletes who have excelled in their chosen sports. Biographical information is included for Chris Evert, Dorothy Hamill, Nadia Comaneci, Kathy Kusner, Cindy Nelson, and Judy Rankin.

17 JACKSON, MADELINE MANNING, with JENKINS, JERRY B. *Running for Jesus*. Waco, Tex.: Word, 192 pp.
Describes Manning's early childhood years and the beginning of her athletic career as a runner. Details her major successes achieved as a runner and the problems she faced attaining those goals. Stresses the importance of her devout religion in her personal life and in her athletic career.

18 JOHNSON, WILLIAM O., and WILLIAMSON NANCY *Whatta Gal! The Babe Didrikson Story*. Boston: Little, Brown, 224 pp.
Chronicles Didrikson's rise to athletic stardom; highlights the outstanding sports conquests that led many to declare her to be the greatest woman athlete in history. Much of the information was gathered from personal interviews with individuals who knew her intimately—her older sister, Lillie; physical education teacher, Bea Lytle; Olympic teammates, Evelyne Hall and Jean Shiley; and good friend and protege, Betty Dodd. Includes personal reflections on both her life and athletic career.

19   JORDAN, PAT. *Broken Patterns*. New York: Dodd, Mead & Co., 213 pp.

       Portrays several different sportswomen representative of the lesser known and less publicized activities in which women participate. Brief descriptions of the athletes and selected incidents in their sports careers are included for Willye White, track; Lillian Ellison, wrestler; Anne Henning, speed skater; Natalie Kahn, Cyndy Groffman, and Shirley Patterson, weight lifters; Shirley Muldowney, drag racer; and Joan Joyce and Donna Lopiano, softball. A more detailed account of the volleyball career of superstar winner Mary Jo Peppler is presented.

20   KURTZ, AGNES BIXLER. *Women's Lacrosse*. Hanover, N.H.: ABK Publications, 132 pp.

       Provides analysis of fundamental and advanced skills and strategies; includes a history of lacrosse. A special section on techniques of coaching discusses conditioning, assessing the players and the game, and psychological factors of competition. Concludes with a summary of the rules of the game.

21   LANCE, KATHRYN. *Running for Health and Beauty*. Indianapolis: Bobbs-Merrill Co., 207 pp.

       Presents detailed information for the woman who wants to begin a running program. Includes what to wear, where and when to run, techniques of running, running injuries and how to avoid them, advice for getting started, and long-distance competitive running. Provides information on the special aspects of menstruation, pregnancy, problems of older women, and dangers faced by women.

22   LEE, MABEL. *Memories of a Bloomer Girl, 1894-1924*. Washington, D.C.: American Alliance for Health, Physical Education, and Recreation, 384 pp.

       Chronicles the first half of Mabel Lee's professional career in physical education. Based on the personal experiences of the author and written in the form of memoirs, it relates the role played by one woman in advancing sports and physical education for women in the United States at a time when the profession was new and women who entered it were pioneers. Humorous anecdotes are interspersed with the more serious aspects of the book which details Lee's career from her early school days to 1924. Is representative of the lives of many women who entered the profession of physical education in its early stages.

23 LIBMAN, GARY. *Lynne Cox*. Mankato, Minn.: Creative Educational Society, 31 pp.

Sketches the accomplishments of teenage channel swimmer Lynne Cox. Provides brief accounts of her swims in channels all over the world interspersed with some of her own thoughts about long-distance swimming.

24 LUCHSINGER, JUDITH A.H. *Practical Self-Defense for Women*. Minneapolis: Dillon Press, 78 pp.

Suggests basic techniques for protection from assault, using judo skills. Describes pressure points and vulnerable areas, techniques for escaping from an assailant, falling, and throwing an attacker. Offers suggestions for preventing attack and developing a mental preparedness for self-protection.

25 McMILLAN, CONSTANCE V. *Nadia Comaneci: Enchanted Sparrow*. St. Paul: EMC Corp., 40 pp.

Describes Comaneci's brief, but highly successful career as a gymnast. Outlines major events in her life from the time she was selected for coaching to her seven perfect scores for performances in the 1976 Olympic Games.

26 MIKLOWITZ, GLORIA D. *Nadia Comaneci*. New York: Grosset & Dunlap, 90 pp.

Highlights the events leading to Comaneci's championship performance in the 1976 Olympic Games.

27 NEFF, FRED. *Self-Protection Guidebook for Girls and Women*. Minneapolis: Lerner Publications Co., 63 pp.

Offers suggestions for avoiding potential trouble; presents self-defense skills in a simple series of learning steps. Describes fighting stances for self-protection; defending against attack with blocks, punches, and kicks; and escaping from attack.

28   O'SHEA, MARY JO. *Winning Tennis Star: Chris Evert*. Mankato, Minn.: Creative Educational Society, 31 pp.

Presents a brief biographical sketch of Evert, focusing primarily on her life and personality rather than on the major competitions in her tennis career.

29   PEPPLER, MARY JO. *Inside Volleyball for Women*. Chicago: Henry Regnery Co., 90 pp.

Designed to help the beginning volleyball player develop skill and to promote the right mind-set needed to become a competitive player. Includes analysis of the techniques of volleyball and suggestions for developing winning play. Regularly directs encouraging comments to the reader.

30   PHILLIPS, BETTY LOU. *Chris Evert, First Lady of Tennis*. New York: Julian Messner, 189 pp.

Chronicles Evert's rise to tennis fame beginning with lessons from her father at the age of six to her attainment of the title world's top-ranked woman tennis player. Intersperses her early triumphs as a young amateur, her move into the professional ranks, and her success as a money-making tennis player with brief glimpses into her personal life.

31   SABIN, FRANCENE. *Set Point, The Story of Chris Evert*. New York: G.P. Putnam's Sons, 127 pp.

Describes Evert's introduction to tennis and her achievements as a young champion, including the warm family relationship in the Evert household and the continuing support provided by her parents. Focuses on her successful rise to championship status and her move into the professional ranks at the age of eighteen.

32   SAUSER, JEAN, and SHAY, ARTHUR. *Inside Racquetball for Women*. Chicago: Contemporary Books, 107 pp.

Presents common errors for racquetball in narrative and photographs; provides corrections for the errors on the facing page. Covers both basic skills and game strategy. Summarizes game rules; includes a glossary of racquetball terms.

33 SCHMITZ, DOROTHY CHILDERS. *Chris Evert: Women's Tennis Champion*. Mankato, Minn.: Crestwood House, 47 pp.

Briefly details Evert's life from her early interest in tennis at the age of seven to her winning the Triple Crown of Women's Tennis in 1976.

34 ____. *Dorothy Hamill, Skate to Victory*. Mankato, Minn.: Crestwood House, 47 pp.

Details Hamill's rise to stardom as a figure skater; relates the dedication and desire necessary to become an amateur champion and her subsequent entry into professional skating.

35 SIMRI, URIEL. *A Historical Analysis of the Role of Women in the Modern Olympic Games*. Natanya, Israel: Wingate Institute for Physical Education and Sport, 50 pp.

Provides a brief history of women's involvement in the Olympic Games and identifies the changing nature of the activities in which women participate. Discusses the growth in participation by women and the current status of their involvement.

36 SMITH, JAY H. *Rosi Mittermaier*. Mankato, Minn.: Creative Educational Society, 31 pp.

Focuses primarily on Mittermaier's performance at the 1976 Winter Olympic Games. Describes her experiences in winning three medals at the age of twenty-five, when most women skiers have retired from major competition.

37 SMITH, MIRANDA A. *Dorothy Hamill*. Mankato, Minn.: Creative Educational Society, 31 pp.

Describes Hamill's gold medal performance at the 1976 Olympic Games; provides a brief description of her training to become a champion.

38 SOUCHERAY, JOE. *Sheila Young*. Mankato, Minn.: Creative Educational Society, 31 pp.

Describes the career highlights of champion speed skater Sheila Young, the first American to win three medals in the Winter Olympics.

39   SPERBER, PAULA, with PEZZANO, CHUCK. *Inside Bowling for Women*. Chicago: Contemporary Books, 74 pp.
    Presents advice about skill performance; discusses appropriate dress, selecting equipment, conditioning exercises, league and tournament competition, and situations such as pregnancy that make bowling different for women.

40   SULLIVAN, GEORGE. *Better Gymnastics for Girls*. New York: Dodd, Mead & Co., 62 pp.
    Provides simple instructions for the basic skills of the balance beam, uneven bars, floor exercise, and vaulting. Includes a brief history of gymnastics.

41   _____. *The Picture Story of Nadia Comaneci*. New York: Julian Messner, 64 pp.
    Sketches the highlights in the short career of Nadia Comaneci, the youngest gymnastics champion in the history of the Olympic Games, and the first person to achieve a judge's perfect score of ten.

42   TAYLOR, PAULA. *Gymnastics' Happy Superstar, Olga Korbut*. Mankato, Minn.: Creative Educational Society, 31 pp.
    Details Korbut's major gymnastic achievements in competition and some of the difficult maneuvers she performs.

43   TEGNER, BRUCE, and McGRATH, ALICE. *Self-Defense and Assault Prevention for Girls and Women*. Ventura, Calif.: Thor Publishing Co., 125 pp.
    Outlines a step-by-step procedure for learning self-defense techniques for a variety of situations. Offers suggestions for preventing situations in which assault could occur.

44   WACHTEL, ERNA, and LOKEN, NEWTON C. *Girls' Gymnastics*. New York: Sterling Publishing Co., 94 pp.
    Analyzes basic techniques for the four competitive events in women's gymnastics: the balance beam, uneven bars, vaulting, and floor exercise. Includes instructions for the even parallel bars, although not a competitive event for women.

45 WALTER, CLAIRE. *Women in Sports: Skiing*. New York: Harvey House, 63 pp.

Presents brief highlights in the ski racing careers of Barbara Ann Cochran, Annemarie Moser-Proell, Cindy Nelson, and cross-country racer Jana Hlavaty. Describes the new competitive event, freestyle or "hot dog" skiing; notes the accomplishments of Suzy Chaffee, Judy Nagel, and Genia Fuller in this professional skiing event.

46 WEIR, MARIE. *Hockey Coaching, A Psychological Approach to the Women's Game*. London: Kaye & Ward, 187 pp.

Departs from the usual skill and strategy analysis of a sport; focuses on the application of psychological theories to coaching field hockey. Includes information on players' needs, team selection, role of the captain, coach-player relationships, group dynamics, aggression, and the implications of working with an all-female team.

1978

1 ADLER, LARRY. *Young Women in the World of Race Horses*. New York: David McKay Co., 56 pp.

Describes the kinds of job possibilities available for women in the world of horse racing and the training and qualifications necessary for them. Includes brief sketches of several well-known women jockeys; discusses harness racers, trainers, and owners of thoroughbreds who are women.

2 BARRILLEAUX, DORIS, and MURRAY, JIM. *Inside Weight Training for Women*. Chicago: Contemporary Books, 69 pp.

Clarifies the differences between weight training and weight lifting; presents a basic exercise program for women using weights. Includes techniques for general conditioning and exercises for special areas of the body.

3 BATEMAN, PY. *Fear into Anger: A Manual of Self-Defense for Women*. Chicago: Nelson-Hall, 133 pp.

Explains techniques that may be useful to women in case of personal attack. Discusses rape prevention and responses to attack in difficult situations such as multiple attackers.

4   BENYO, RICH, ed. *The Complete Woman Runner*. Mountain View, Calif.: World Publications, 443 pp.

   Covers virtually everything an aspiring runner may wish to know. Includes information on training; dealing with a family; safety for female runners; anatomical, cardiorespiratory, and psychological aspects of running; and progressing beyond jogging. Describes the pioneering efforts of Roberta Gibb, Kathy Switzer, Nina Kuscsik, and Sara Berman in long-distance running. Includes brief profiles of fifty American women who run, the average runners who may train a minimum of a mile and a half per day and those who may run one hundred miles a week.

5   BONING, RICHARD A. *Glenda's Long Swim*. Baldwin, N.Y.: Dexter & Westbrook, 47 pp.

   Sketches Glenda Lennon's struggles to stay afloat twenty hours until her rescue after being towed away from her boat by strong currents while snorkeling in the Gulf of Mexico.

6   BORSTEIN, LARRY. *After Olympic Glory*. New York: Frederick Warne, 185 pp.

   Presents biographical sketches of four Olympic athletes, focusing on their activities after competing in the Games. Includes Micki King (pp. 19-33), Donna deVarona (pp. 69-87), Tenley Albright (pp. 105-119), and Nell Jackson (pp. 153-167).

7   BOULOGNE, JEAN. *The Making of A Gymnast*. New York: Hawthorn Books, 96 pp.

   Describes the hard work, dedication, and commitment required to excel as a gymnast. Focuses on the development of Karen Kelsall from her early training to her status as an elite gymnast.

8   BRACKENRIDGE, CELIA. *Women's Lacrosse*. Woodbury, N.Y.: Barron's Educational Series, 60 pp.

   Provides detailed analyses of fundamental skills; discusses offensive and defensive strategy; suggests ideas for effective use of practice time.

9   BURCHARD, SUE H. *Sports Star, Dorothy Hamill*. New York: Harcourt Brace Jovanovich, 63 pp.

Highlights the skating career of Dorothy Hamill from her first skates at the age of eight to her gold medal performance in the 1976 Olympic Games. Describes the training and discipline necessary for becoming a champion.

10   CAHILL, WILLY. *Kick and Run*. Burbank, Cal.: Ohara Publications, 95 pp.

Describes techniques for protecting oneself from personal attack. Focuses primarily on kicks from the martial arts, with advice for disrupting an attack and getting away as quickly as possible.

11   CLAFLIN, EDWARD. *The Irresistible American Softball Book*. Garden City, N.Y.: Doubleday & Co., 128 pp.

Weaves an interesting story of factual information about the game of softball into such provocative topics as "Softball Power," "Underhand Combat," and "I'll Flip You for Shifty." Information about women is interwoven throughout the book, with a special section devoted to the establishment of the professional All-American Girls Baseball League in 1943.

12   COAKLEY, JAY J. "Women in Sport, Separate or Equal." In *Sport in Society: Issues and Controversies*. St. Louis: C. V. Mosby Co., pp. 243-273.

Focuses on cultural definitions of sport and sex roles and the impact of these on women's sport participation. Offers suggestions for changing those definitions in order to move toward equality of opportunity for women in sport.

13   COOK, JOSEPH J. *Famous Firsts in Tennis*. New York: G. P. Putnam's Sons, 63 pp.

Provides brief biographical information about individuals who were "firsts" in tennis. Women included are Ellen Hansell, Women's National Singles Champion; May Sutton, American winner at Wimbledon; Hazel Wightman, donor of the Wightman Cup; Suzanne Lenglen, stylist on the court; Helen Wills, Wightman Cup winner; Maureen Connolly, female "grand slam" winner; Althea Gibson, first black to win a major championship; Margaret Court, winner of ten

Australian national crowns; and Billie Jean King, player who had a great effect on society's views about women.

14 COSTANZA, BETTY, with GLOSSBRENNER, ALFRED. *Women's Track and Field*. New York: Hawthorn Books, 163 pp.

Directed toward the beginning athlete in a style that could be used for self-learning. Presents techniques for warming up and proper conditioning; includes enough skill analysis for learning acceptable performance.

15 COULTON, JILL. *Women's Gymnastics*. Wakefield, West Yorkshire, England: E.P. Publishing, 116 pp.

Analyzes skills for performing on the beam, horse, bars, and in floor exercise, the competitive events for women. Includes a series of basic exercises for warm-up activities; is profusely illustrated with photographs and drawings.

16 COVINO, MARGE, and JORDAN, PAT. *Woman's Guide to Shaping your Body with Weights*. Philadelphia: J.B. Lippincott Co., 175 pp.

Examines the myths about weight lifting for women; offers a program of body building through the use of weights and weight machines. Outlines routines for achieving various fitness goals and proper diet to supplement the body building routine.

17 DOLAN, EDWARD F., Jr., and LYTTLE, RICHARD B. *Janet Guthrie, First Woman Driver at Indianapolis*. Garden City, N.Y.: Doubleday & Co., 80 pp.

Describes Guthrie's early life, her interest in flying, followed by her interest in auto racing, which culminated in her qualifying as the first woman driver in the Indianapolis 500.

18 EITZEN, D. STANLEY, and SAGE, GEORGE H. "Females in American Sport: Continuity and Change." In *Sociology of American Sport*. Dubuque, Iowa: William C. Brown Co., pp. 261-287.

Examines the sociologically significant role of women in American sport; identifies prevailing myths and attitudes about women's participation in sport; briefly touches on the relationship of the women's liberation movement to sport.

19   FLEDER, HELEN. *Shower Power*. New York: M. Evans & Co., 149 pp.

Contains a collection of exercises designed to be performed in the bathroom using either the shower, tub, or bathroom floor space. Provides instructions and illustrations for each exercise.

20   FLINT, RACHEL HEYWOOD. *Field Hockey*. Woodbury, N.Y.: Barron's Educational Series, 64 pp.

Covers basic skills, tactics, and rules for playing field hockey; written for beginning players.

21   GLICKMAN, WILLIAM G. *Winners on the Tennis Court*. New York: Franklin Watts, 48 pp.

Presents highlights in the careers of Chris Evert, Evonne Goolagong, and Billie Jean King.

22   GOLDEN, FLORA. *Women in Sports: Horseback Riding*. New York: Harvey House, 70 pp.

Presents a brief history of women's involvement in horseback riding; explains types of riding competition. Includes biographical sketches for jockey Denise Boudrot; jumper Michele McEvoy; dressage rider Hilda Gurney; polo player Sue Sally Jones; and show rider, coach, and trainer Helen Crabtree.

23   HAHN, JAMES, and HAHN, LYNN. *Janet Guthrie: Champion Racer*. St. Paul: EMC Corp., 40 pp.

Focuses on the career of Janet Guthrie, the first woman driver to qualify for the Indianapolis 500 auto race. Describes her early life and the struggles she faced in attempting to break into the masculine domain of auto racing.

24   HUNT, LESLEY. *Inside Tennis for Women*. Chicago: Contemporary Books, 133 pp.

Attempts to deal with the special attributes and demands of tennis that are different from those of the men's game. Analyzes game skills in detail, clarifies analysis with photographs and diagrams. Describes strategy for both singles and doubles play; offers suggestions for developing concentration and handling nerves in competitive play. Concludes with basic information on scoring and court etiquette.

25   ITO, ROBERT, and DOLNEY, PAM CHILLA. *Mastering Women's Gymnastics*. Chicago: Contemporary Books, 160 pp.

Provides an overall view of the requirements for the sport of gymnastics. Exercises and fundamental skills for warming up are followed by analysis of skills for the four competitive events for women – floor exercise, vaulting, balance beam, and uneven bars. Describes spotting techniques; is amply illustrated with sequential photographs and drawings.

26   JACOBS, KAREN FOLGER. *Girlsports*. New York: Bantam Books, 187 pp.

Describes the achievements of fifteen young female athletes in a variety of activities ranging from jacks to rodeo. Some, such as Tai Babilonia, Olympic skater, are well known; others may never be known outside their own local community. Each, however, has been a successful competitor and knows what it is like to be the only girl on a boys' team, to work long, grueling hours to become a champion, and to feel the real joy that comes from sports participation.

27   JONES, BILLIE J., and MURRAY, MARY JO. *Softball: Concepts for Teachers and Coaches*. Dubuque, Iowa: William C. Brown Co., 215 pp.

Presents a history of softball; defines the slow-pitch and fast-pitch games. Analyzes skills of the game and offensive and defensive strategies; includes practice drills and teaching-learning tips for each of the specialized positions. Offers detailed advice for the purchase and care of equipment and uniforms, conditioning, teaching, and coaching.

28   KLAFS, CARL E., and LYON, M. JOAN. *The Female Athlete*, St. Louis: C.V. Mosby, 351 pp.

Focuses on a means of preventing injury but includes information in a variety of other areas. A brief history of women's participation in sports introduces the book, and remaining sections cover anthropometric and physiological factors in sport performance; physical conditioning; and sports training that is primarily concerned with care and prevention of injuries. Chapters are included in the last section, however, on nutrition and athletic performance and the facts and fallacies pertaining to ergogenic aids. A special feature of the book is the inclusion of individual training programs of several champion athletes in a variety of sports.

29   KREMENTZ, JILL. *A Very Young Gymnast*. New York: Alfred A. Knopf, 119 pp.

   Relates the events in the training and life of a gymnast; accompanying photographs provide excellent illustrations of the activities of a budding gymnast.

30   ____. *A Very Young Rider*. New York: Alfred A. Knopf, 119 pp.

   Relates ideas about horses and riding through the eyes of a ten-year old. Describes responsibilities in caring for and owning a horse and the hard work and dedication necessary to become a competitive rider. Excellent photographs provide as much information as the narrative.

31   KURTZ, AGNES B. *Women's Lacrosse, for Coaches and Players*. Hanover, N.H.: ABK Publications, 132 pp.

   Focuses primarily on advanced skills and strategies for use by coaches. Includes fundamental skill analysis; discusses conditioning, assessing the players and the game, and psychological factors related to competition.

32   LANCE, KATHRYN. *Getting Strong: A Woman's Guide to Realizing her Physical Potential*. Indianapolis: Bobbs-Merrill Co., 238 pp.

   Presents a program for developing and maintaining body strength. Includes information on diet and figure control and how to improve sport performance through strength training.

33   LEE, MABEL. *Memories Beyond Bloomers, 1924-1955*. Washington, D.C.: American Alliance for Health, Physical Education, and Recreation, 474 pp.

Is a sequel to *Memories of a Bloomer Girl* (1977) and continues the story of Lee's professional career in physical education up to the time of her retirement in 1954. She writes from first-hand experience of her work in various professional organizations, her insights into the organizational politics of such groups, and her tenure as the first woman president of the American Physical Education Association. Of particular interest are her descriptions of early developments in athletics for women and the continuing controversies surrounding them. This continuation of memories offers unusual insights into the development of physical education for women and the early days of women's athletics.

34   LUCAS, JOHN A., and SMITH, RONALD A. "From Corsets to Bloomers–Women in Sport." In *Saga of American Sport*. Philadelphia: Lea and Febiger, pp. 250-266.

Focuses on the development of sport for women in the United States from mid-nineteenth century up to the early 1900s with special emphasis on the college-educated woman and the role of the bicycle in sport for women.

35   ____. "Women's Sport: A Trial of Equality." In *Saga of American Sport*. Philadelphia: Lea and Febiger, pp. 342-372.

Emphasizes the development of women's sport after World War I, clarifying the "women's anticompetitive movement" in the 1920s, 1930s, and 1940s when high level competition was frowned upon. Describes the revolution in women's sports that was occurring after World War II.

36   MIKLOWITZ, GLORIA D. *Tracy Austin*. New York: Grossett & Dunlap, 87 pp.

Details the brief career of tennis star Tracy Austin, the youngest player to compete at Wimbledon. Describes the tennis successes of the entire Austin family of parents, an older sister, and three older brothers, and Tracy's quick rise to championship status.

37   NEAL, PATSY. *Coaching Methods for Women*, Reading, Mass.: Addison-Wesley Publishing Co., 294 pp.

Written primarily for coaches of girls' and women's sports and includes chapters on the role of the coach, factors in coaching women, and prerequisites for champions as well as the practical aspects of coaching such as organizing and selecting the team, training and conditioning, and planning for a sports season. Provides skill and strategy analyses and coaching suggestions for twelve different sports. Offers diverse information concerning the coaching of women, and the author's own philosophy of coaching is evident in many of the chapters.

38   NYAD, DIANA. *Other Shores*. New York: Random House, 174 pp.
         Provides a personal account of Nyad's record-setting achievements as a marathon swimming champion. Explains the in-depth training required for her accomplishments and the sensory deprivation and almost hypnotic sensation that occurs in long-distance swims. Details the preparation for her highly publicized swim from Havana, Cuba, to Marathon, Florida.

39   OLGESBY, CAROLE A. *Women and Sport: From Myth to Reality*. Philadelphia: Lea and Febiger, 268 pp.
         Contains a series of papers by several different authors, all women; is described by the author as a book about sports feminism. It is, however, a provocative collection of material that explores a variety of subjects concerned with the female and sport. A brief history of women's participation in sport introduces the book and is followed by thirteen chapters set in the framework of sections titled "Society and the Female Body;" "Society, Sport, and Sexuality;" "Society, Sport Involvement, and Sport Achievement;" and "Women's Sport: Myth, Reality, and Social Change." Most chapters have detailed bibliographies. While the book may appear to be strongly slanted toward the feminist viewpoint, the author has provided an excellent collection of theoretical and practical information about the problems and the positive aspects that evolve from women's sports participation

40   OLNEY, ROSS R. *Janet Guthrie, First Woman to Race at Indy*. New York: Harvey House, 54 pp.
         Traces the life and auto racing career of Janet Guthrie, a physicist whose goal was to race in the Indianapolis 500, achieved in 1978.

41   ROBISON, NANCY. *Tracy Austin, Teenage Superstar*. New York: Harvey House, 63 pp.

Details the brief life and career of tennis player Tracy Austin, her early interest in tennis, and her major accomplishments as an amateur player.

42   SABIN, LOUIS. *100 Great Moments in Sports*. New York: G.P. Putnam's Sons, 191 pp.

Includes brief biographical information for a number of women athletes; focuses primarily on a great moment in the career of the athlete such as Nadia Comaneci's seven perfect scores at the 1976 Olympic Games and Gertrude Ederle's English Channel swim.

43   SCHOOR, GENE. *Babe Didrikson: The World's Greatest Woman Athlete*. Garden City, N.Y.: Doubleday & Co., 185 pp.

Describes Didrikson's early childhood; focuses primarily on her many and diverse accomplishments as a sports champion. Emphasizes her life and relationship with husband, George Zaharias. Includes a list of her championship records in track and golf.

44   SNYDER, ELDON E., and SPREITZER, ELMER A. "The Female Athlete." In *Social Aspects of Sport*. Englewood Cliffs, N.J.: Prentice-Hall, pp. 105-121.

Examines the relationship between sex roles and women's involvement in athletics. Briefly discusses the psychological dimensions of women's athletic participation; concludes with a brief historical commentary.

45   SPEARS, BETTY, and SWANSON, RICHARD A. *History of Sport and Physical Activity in the United States*. Dubuque, Iowa: William C. Brown Co., 414 pp.

Divides the development of sport and physical activity into six time periods from 1492 to 1975 and includes a discussion of women's activities for each of the periods as well as some discussion of women in the Olympic Games in a final chapter.

46   SULLIVAN, GEORGE. *Better Basketball for Girls*. New York: Dodd, Mead & Co., 64 pp.

Discusses history of women's basketball; presents skill analysis, techniques of the game, and offensive and defensive strategy; includes a summary of rules. Is illustrated with photographs, including several of historical interest from 1895 to the 1930s.

47 TYUS, WYOMIA. *Inside Jogging for Women*. Chicago: Contemporary Books, 60 pp.
    Written for the general reader interested in running as exercise for fitness rather than competition. Describes the basics of beginning a jogging program and techniques for running.

48 VAN STEENWYK, ELIZABETH. *Peggy Fleming: Cameo of a Champion*. New York: McGraw-Hill Book Co., 132 pp.
    Presents the story of Fleming's career as an amateur figure skater, beginning with her transition from violin lessons to skating lessons and progressing through the various experiences in her rise to championship status. Describes the major competitions in which she participated, concluding with her gold-medal victory in the 1968 Olympic Games.

49 _____. *Women in Sports: Rodeo*. New York: Harvey House, 78 pp.
    Presents a brief history of the development of rodeo for women; describes the seven standard events in which women compete. Sketches the rodeo activities of several young competitors.

50 WADE, VIRGINIA, with WALLACE, MARY LOU. *Courting Triumph*. New York: Mayflower Books, 192 pp.
    Provides a detailed account of Wade's 1977 win at Wimbledon, a provocative study of the thoughts and feelings of a top-flight player under pressure of the final match on center court. Includes interesting tales of her personal life, her rise to tennis success, and her problem with self-direction and developing the strong will to win so necessary for achieving success.

51 WALSH, LOREN. *Contemporary Softball*. Chicago: Contemporary Books, 122 pp.
    Begins with a history of softball and the differences in the fast- and slow-pitch games. Includes skill analysis and strategy for playing the game. Usable for either women's or men's softball.

52 WILLIAMS, LEE ANN. *Basic Field Hockey Strategy*. Garden City, N.Y.: Doubleday & Co., 105 pp.

Discusses individual skills, defensive and offensive strategies, game rules, practice drills, and conditioning. Is primarily an introduction to field hockey for beginning players.

53 WILT, FRED; ECKER, TOM; and HAY, JIM, eds. *Championship Track and Field for Women*. West Nyack, N.Y.: Parker Publishing Co., 270 pp.

Analyzes each of the nine track and field events in which women participate; written by contributors recognized for their expertise in the particular event. Focuses on coaching techniques for skilled performers; includes information on the biomechanical, physiological, and sociopsychological aspects of the female competitor.

1979

1 ADOFF, ARNOLD. *I Am the Running Girl*. New York: Harper Row, 35 pp.

Describes the joy of running, using poetry as the medium. Illustrated with drawings by artist Ronald Himler.

2 ALDERMAN, CLIFFORD LINDSEY. *Annie Oakley and the World of Her Time*. New York: Macmillan Publishing Co., 91 pp.

Details Oakley's early life and her career as a successful performer and markswoman in the wild west shows of the nineteenth century.

3 ASCH, FRANK, and ASCH, JAN. *Running with Rachel*. New York: Dial Press, 64 pp.

Describes the experiences of a young girl, in her own words, as she develops an interest in running and begins to run on a regular basis.

4 BACKUS, SHARRON. *Inside Softball for Women*. Chicago: Contemporary Books, 88 pp.

Discusses the nature of softball; analyzes playing skills and team strategy in specific situations. Includes coaching suggestions.

5   BARTHOL, ROBERT G. *Protect Yourself: A Self-Defense Guide for Women from Prevention to Counterattack*. Englewood Cliffs, N.J.: Prentice-Hall, 234 pp.
    Presents clear and simple explanations for women's self-protection; includes preventive measures as well as defensive maneuvers in case of attack. Focuses primarily on simple self-defense techniques rather than skills learned from the martial arts. Is generously illustrated.

6   BURG, KATHLEEN KEEFE. *The Womanly Art of Self-Defense*. New York: A & W Visual Library, 175 pp.
    Describes commonsense ways of dealing with personal attack; explains how to use self-defense moves; suggests techniques for avoiding the possibility of attack.

7   COOPER, GWEN, and HAAS, EVELYN. *Wade A Little Deeper, Dear*. San Francisco: California Living Books, 107 pp.
    Provides a guide to fly-fishing written specifically for women. Includes information on the basics of fishing etiquette, the use of wet and dry flies, how to tie knots, and easy recipes for cooking the "catch."

8   DOLAN, EDWARD F., Jr., and LYTTLE, RICHARD B. *Dorothy Hamill, Olympic Skating Champion*. Garden City, N.Y.: Doubleday & Co., 95 pp.
    Focuses on Hamill's career as a figure skater and Olympic gold medalist.

9   ENGLANDER, JOE, *They Ride the Rodeo: The Men and Women of the American Amateur Rodeo Circuit*. New York: Collier Books, 126 pp.
    Presents a photo story of rodeo events with a brief descriptive first person narrative by the author/photographer about his experiences with the rodeo.

10 FAULKNER, MARGARET. *I Skate!* Boston: Little, Brown & Co., 154 pp.

Follows the experiences of eleven-year-old Karen Berig and her aspirations to become a champion figure skater. Details her daily training sessions and her participation in competition.

11   FILSON, SIDNEY. *How to Protect Yourself and Survive, From One Woman to Another*. New York: Franklin Watts, 158 pp.
     Discusses basic techniques for self-protection including the use of weapons. Suggests ways of dealing with specific situations and for protecting oneself from rape.

12   FRAYNE, TRENT. *Famous Women Tennis Players*. New York: Dodd, Mead & Co., 223 pp.
     Presents biographical data concerning the lives and careers of tennis greats Suzanne Lenglen, Helen Wills, Helen Jacobs, Alice Marble, Maureen Connolly, Margaret Court, Althea Gibson, Virginia Wade, Evonne Goolagong, Billie Jean King, Chris Evert, and Martina Navratilova.

13   GALUB, JACK. *The United States Air Force Academy Fitness Program for Women*. Englewood Cliffs, N.J.: Prentice-Hall, 219 pp.
     Describes the fitness program for women at the United States Air Force Academy. Explains how the program was designed and instituted; includes instructions for general conditioning exercises and cardiovascular training. A section on women and sports describes the Academy's athletic program and offers suggestions for participation in a variety of other sports. A final section focuses on special topics such as self-motivation, stress, and depression and the relationship of these to activity.

14   GROS, VONNIE. *Inside Field Hockey for Women*. Chicago: Contemporary Books, 102 pp.
     Analyzes skills and tactics necessary to play competitive field hockey; includes condition for the hockey player. Reflects the increasing interest in the United States in highly competitive hockey play.

15   GUTMAN, BILL. *More Modern Women Superstars*. New York: Dodd, Mead & Co., 125 pp.

Presents brief biographical sketches of five athletes who have been successful in their respective sports. Includes Tracy Austin, Carol Blazejowski, Janet Guthrie, Joan Joyce, and Nancy Lopez.

16   HAHN, JAMES, and HAHN, LYNN. *Nancy Lopez, Golfing Pioneer.* St. Paul: EMC Corporation, 40 pp.

Describes the early life and amateur participation of Nancy Lopez, the first Mexican American to achieve success on the Ladies Professional Golfer's Association (LPGA) tour. Concludes with her experiences after becoming a professional golfer in 1977.

17   HANEY, LYNN. *Perfect Balance: The Story of an Elite Gymnast.* New York: G.P. Putnam's Sons, 60 pp.

Describes the training of Leslie Russo as she works toward achieving success in gymnastics competition.

18   HURT, MARCIA. *Inside Basketball for Women.* Chicago: Contemporary Books, 102 pp.

Directed primarily toward the competitive player and coach; includes conditioning, individual and team offensive and defensive tactics. Concludes with suggestions for developing positive relationships between coach and players and among team members.

19   KAPLAN, JANICE. *Women and Sports: Inspiration and Information for the New Female Athlete.* New York: Viking Press, 204 pp.

Provides an overview of the current sport scene for women in a style written for the general reader. Covers a variety of topics including physiological aspects of sport for women, nutrition, selecting one's sport, and competition. Promotes integrated sports for women and men whenever possible, but notes a particular concern that women's sports of the future not be modeled after the men's sports programs.

20   LIGHTHALL, NANCY; STENMARK, PAMELA; with ABRAHAM, HORST. *Skiing for Women.* Palm Springs, Calif.: ETC Publications, 122 pp.

Details the information deemed by the authors to be necessary to get started in skiing and achieve success with it. Includes teaching techniques, getting in shape, common errors and corrections, and suggestions for deep snow skiing. Concludes with recommended courtesies to be exercised by the skier.

21 LOPEZ, NANCY, and SCHWED, PETER. *The Education of a Woman Golfer*. New York: Simon & Schuster, 191 pp.
      Presents autobiographical details of Lopez's education in golf; offers her view of the sport and competing in it. Though technically not an instructional manual, techniques and hints for improving one's game are scattered throughout the book. Offers brief biographical sketches of many of Lopez's competitors.

22 MADDUX, GORDON, and SHAY, ARTHUR. *40 Common Errors in Women's Gymnastics and How to Correct Them*. Chicago: Contemporary Books, 106 pp.
      Focuses on common errors in gymnastics; describes the mistake and the correction for it. Illustrates each error and correction with a photograph.

23 MARTIN, ANN. *The Equestrian Woman*. New York: Grossett & Dunlap, 224 pp.
      Presents brief biographical sketches of twenty-one equestriennes who participate in diverse activities from racing to driving. Emphasis is placed on riders in racing, hunting, and dressage events.

24 McWHIRTER, NORRIS; MORGENSTERN, STEVE; MORGENSTERN, ROZ; and GREENBERG, STAN. *Guinness Book of Women's Sports Records*. New York: Sterling Publishing Co., 192 pp.
      Provides factual information and records of winners for forty-six different activities, including some unusual ones such as bull fighting and parachute jumping. Statistical information for each sport is preceded by a brief informational paragraph about the activity.

25 MORAN, LYN. *The Young Gymnasts*. New York: K.S. Giniger Co., 239 pp.
      Focuses on a number of young women from around the world who are developing into elite competitive gymnasts. Briefly describes

some of their achievements to date and some of the intricacies of gymnastics competition.

26 MURRAY, MIMI. *Women's Gymnastics*. Boston: Allyn & Bacon, 289 pp.

Offers a comprehensive view of gymnastics for women. Chapters for each competitive event provide skill analysis, teaching techniques, skill progressions, and corrections for common errors. Examines the coaching role, offering special advice for the person in the position. Covers basic as well as advanced skill levels; is well illustrated with both photographs and drawings.

27 PHILLIPS, LOUIS, and MARKOE, KAREN. *Women in Sports, Records, Stars, Feats and Facts*. New York: Harcourt Brace Jovanovich, 174 pp.

Presents brief biographical facts for thirty-five women athletes, ranging from Helen Wills and Gertrude Ederle in the 1920s to Nadia Comaneci and Chris Evert of the 1970s, followed by a collection of facts and figures pertaining to virtually every sport in which women participate.

28 PICKERING, MICHAEL G.V. *A Woman's Self-Defense Manual*. Mountain View, Calif.: World Publications, 143 pp.

Focuses on both physical and nonphysical approaches for protecting oneself from personal attack.

29 PRESTIDGE, JIM. *The Love of Gymnastics*. New York: Crescent Books, 96 pp.

Presents a brief history of the development of gymnastics from the Ancient Olympic Games to the present. Discusses the nature of performance on the apparatus used by women and men. Analyzes basic skills used on the apparatus. Is well illustrated with photographs.

30 RILEY, DANIEL P., and PETERSON, JAMES A. *Not for Men Only: Strength Training for Women*. West Point: Leisure Press, 128 pp.

Discusses the myths perpetuated about women and weight training; offers techniques and methods for developing a successful weight training program, both with and without the use of equipment.

31   ROBISON, NANCY. *Janet Guthrie, Race Car Driver*. Chicago: Children's Press, 44 pp.

Details Guthrie's racing experiences at the Indianapolis 500 in the year in which she was a competitor attempting to qualify for the race. Includes information about the two years, 1977 and 1978, in which she did compete.

32   ____. *Nancy Lopez, Wonder of Golf*. Chicago: Children's Press, 42 pp.

Presents a biographical sketch of Nancy Lopez's short, but successful golf career, both as an amateur and a professional.

33   SCHUMACHER, CRAIG. *Nancy Lopez*. Mankato, Minn.: Creative Education, 32 pp.

Outlines Lopez's life and the successes she achieved in her short career as an amateur and professional golfer.

34   SCOTT, M. GLADYS, and HOFEREK, MARY J., eds. *Women as Leaders in Physical Education and Sports*. Iowa City: University of Iowa Press, 79 pp.

Examines the role of women as leaders in sport and physical education and the issues with which they must deal in those roles. Explores institutional variables, politics, and cultural perspectives that impact women as they strive toward leadership roles.

35   SEGHERS, CARROL, II. *The Peak Experience: Hiking and Climbing for Women*. Indianapolis: Bobbs-Merrill Co., 316 pp.

Introduces the reader to both the joys and cautions of mountaineering; includes instructional information on the requirements for the sport from selecting equipment and training to behavior and leadership on the trail. Provides extensive instructions for basic climbing; attempts to dispel some of the myths about the effects of strenuous exercise on women's physique.

36 SIMRI, URIEL. *Women at the Olympic Games*, 2nd ed. Netanya, Israel: Wingate Institute for Physical Education and Sport, 91 pp.

Originally published in 1977 as *A Historical Analysis of the Role of Women in the Modern Olympic Games* (35). Expanded to include a brief chapter on women at ancient Olympia and data from the 1976 Games in Montreal.

37 SLANGER, ELISSA, and WITCHELL, DINAH B. *Ski Woman's Way*. New York: Summit Books, 219 pp.

Presents a woman's approach to learning to ski, identified as the educational program, Woman's Way. Includes information on selection of equipment, overcoming fear, the benefits of skiing, and ski tips designed for women only.

38 SULLIVAN, GEORGE. *Modern Olympic Superstars*. New York: Dodd, Mead & Co., 111 pp.

Briefly details the lives of six Olympic gold medalists, three of them women. Discusses the early lives, entry into high level competition, and some of the competitive successes of Cornelia Ender, Nelli Kim, and Sheila Young.

39 TINGAY, LANCE. *Tennis: A Pictorial History*. London: William Collins Sons & Co., 168 pp.

Presents an amply illustrated history of tennis with excellent photographs dating from the 1870s. Narrative provides an overview of the development of the sport in chronologically organized sections from "The Genesis of a Sport" to "Tennis as Big Business." Approximately half of the photographs are of women.

40 TWIN, STEPHANIE L. *Out of the Bleachers*. Old Westbury, N.Y.: Feminist Press, 229 pp.

Introduced with a brief history of woman's involvement in sport and the societal views of woman's role that have curtailed her participation. The articles that follow in the anthology explore the place of woman in the sports world through both contemporary and historical writings. Separate sections are devoted to physiological aspects and social attitudes, reflections on the lives of selected sportswomen, and the structure of women's sports.

1980

1   BLUM, ARLENE. *Annapurna, A Woman's Place*. San Francisco: Sierra Club Books, 268 pp.

Chronicles the first ascent of Annapurna by a team of American women in 1978. Includes a number of excerpts from the diaries of the climbers, capturing the essence of both the exhilaration and the difficulties of such an endeavor. Notes that the American Women's Himalayan Expedition was not designed "to prove that women could climb high mountains" (p. xi), but the success of the trip, as described by the author, undoubtedly served that purpose and sent that message to others around the world. Concludes with an excellent bibliography on mountaineering.

2   BROWN, JAMES R., and WARDELL, DAVID B. *Teaching and Coaching Gymnastics for Men and Women*. New York: John Wiley & Sons, 455 pp.

Presents a brief history of gymnastics and organizational procedures for developing a program. Analyzes skills and routines for both women's and men's competitive activities. Examines legal liability involved with gymnastics teaching and coaching.

3   CHISAM, SCOTT C. *Inside Track for Women*. Chicago: Contemporary Books, 88 pp.

Focuses on the following women's running events: sprints, hurdles, mid- and long-distance running, and relays. Analyzes techniques for performing each event; suggests practice techniques for each. Includes sample training programs for all events, complemented with a program of drills and plyometrics.

4   COOPER, PHYLLIS. *Feminine Gymnastics*, 3d ed. Minneapolis: Burgess Publishing Co., 316 pp.

First published in 1968 (2), revised in 1973 (3). Third edition reflects changes that have occurred in gymnastics as competition has quickened. Includes information on conditioning and mechanical analysis of movement and additional illustrations of skills not included in prior editions.

5   CRAGG, SHEILA. *Run Patty Run*. San Francisco: Harper & Row, 175 pp.

Chronicles the long-distance running career of epileptic Patty Wilson, and her efforts, through running, to help others understand more about the affliction. Details several of the long runs she made prior to her high school graduation.

6   EDMONDSON, JOLEE. *The Woman Golfer's Catalogue*. New York: Stein & Day, 224 pp.

Offers a potpourri of golfing information for women, only a small part of which is instructional. Discusses equipment, golf apparel, grooming for golf, hair conditioners and shampoos, and sun screens and moisturizers. Approximately half of the book is devoted to biographical sketches of outstanding women players from the early 1900s to 1980. Includes professional tournament records, individual successes, and awards.

7   FOGEL, JULIANNA A., and WATKINS, MARY S. *Andrea Jaeger, Tennis Champion*. New York: J.B. Lippincott, 41 pp.

Outlines Jaeger's brief tennis career in a narrative as if she were telling the story herself. Generously illustrated with photographs, the book should appeal to young tennis enthusiasts.

8   GEORGE, GERALD S. *Biomechanics of Women's Gymnastics*. Englewood Cliffs, N.J.: Prentice-Hall, 236 pp.

Presents general principles for refining gymnastics movements followed by analysis of specific skills performed on the balance beam, uneven bars, in floor exercise, and the vault. Includes spotting and safety procedures; is generously illustrated with drawings

9   HANNA, MIKE. *Lacrosse for Men and Women*. New York: Hawthorn/Dutton, 223 pp.

Introduced as a "book for both men and women" (p. ix), far more emphasis is given to the men's game. Included, however, for the women's game are basic skills, individual and team offense and defense, and practice drills for developing skill. A brief conditioning section is included, as well as a clarification of the differences between the women's and men's games.

10   HAYCOCK, CHRISTINE, ed. *Sports Medicine for the Athletic Female*. Oradell, N.J.: Medical Economics Co., Book Division, 423 pp.

Presents a collection of articles that focus on various aspects of the female athlete. Psychology, injuries and rehabilitation, physiology, nutrition, conditioning, orthopedic problems, gynecological factors, drugs, and cardiovascular considerations are representative of the subject matter covered.

11   KUNTZLEMAN, CHARLES, and CRYDERMAN, LYN. *They Accepted the Challenge*. New York: St. Martin's Press, 263 pp.

Presents a collection of heartwarming stories of persons involved in various forms of sport and exercise who might not usually be expected to do so. Examples of persons who overcame insurmountable odds to achieve their personal goals include Susan Guild, a figure skater with leukemia; Lori Markle, a softball player with an artificial leg; Hulda Crooks, an octogenarian mountain climber; and Jane Tubbs, who returned to racquetball competition ten months after suffering a stroke.

12   LaBASTILLE, ANNE. *Women and Wilderness*. San Francisco: Sierra Club Books, 320 pp.

Examines the historical roles of women who pioneered in the frontier wilderness and profiles fifteen contemporary women who "live full-time or work professionally in the outdoors or have wilderness-oriented careers" (p. 2).

13   LAKLAN, CARLI. *Golden Girls*. New York: McGraw-Hill Co., 164 pp.

Focuses on the Olympic successes of a variety of athletes; includes Tenley Albright, Fanny Blankers-Koen, Donna deVarona, Gertrude Ederle, Peggy Fleming, Dorothy Hamill, Carol Heiss, Sonja Henie, Olga Korbut, Cathy Rigby, Barbara Ann Scott, Wyomia Tyus, Willye White, Helen Wills, and Babe Didrikson Zaharias.

14   LANCE, KATHRYN. *A Woman's Guide to Spectator Sports*. New York: A & W Publishers, 351 pp.

Written as a guide to help women become informed spectators of sports in which they may not normally participate – baseball, football, hockey, basketball, and soccer. A general overview of how the game is played, rules of the game, and officials' signals are explained for each activity.

15 McLENIGHAN, VALJEAN DIANA. *Alone against the Sea*. Milwaukee: Raintree Publishers, 47 pp.
     Presents biographical information on marathon swimmer Diana Nyad. Emphasizes her forty-one hour attempt to swim from Cuba to the Florida coast.

16 McREYNOLDS, GINNY. *Woman Overboard*. Milwaukee: Raintree Publishers, 44 pp.
     Details the events of Glenda Lennon's snorkeling trip in the Gulf of Mexico in which she drifted away from her boat and struggled to remain afloat and alive until her rescue twenty hours later.

17 PARKHOUSE, BONNIE L., and LAPIN, JACKIE. *The Woman in Athletic Administration*. Santa Monica: Goodyear Publishing Co., 335 pp.
     Written as a basic handbook for the woman in athletic administration. Describes a variety of management techniques and offers guidelines for handling the many details that are responsibilities of the athletic administrator. Fund raising, budget planning, health care, public relations, and contest management are but a few of the topics that have lengthy coverage in the book.

18 ____. *Women Who Win: Exercising Your Rights in Sport*. Englewood Cliffs, N. J.: Prentice Hall, 272 pp.
     Focuses on the rights of women in sport and the legitimate ways one may exercise those rights. Practical approaches to problems that arise for women in athletic administration are offered along with suggestions for getting along with male cohorts. Legal avenues that may be used to achieve equality are identified, and actual court decisions are used for clarification.

19 PHILLIPS, BETTY LOU. *The Picture Story of Nancy Lopez*. New York: Julian Messner, 64 pp.

Briefly describes the golf career of Nancy Lopez from her introduction to the game as a child to her successful entry into professional golf.

20   SABO, DONALD F., Jr., and ROSS, RUNFOLA. *Jock: Sports and Male Identity*. Englewood Cliffs, N.J.: Prentice-Hall, 373 pp.
     Examines the issue of masculinity in sport; includes the following essays focusing on women: "Sports, Women and the Ideology of Domination" by Mark Naison (pp. 30-36); "Sport: Women Sit in the Back of the Bus" by M. Marie Hart (pp. 205-211); "The Game is Fixed: Programmed to be Losers" by Thomas Boslooper and Marcia Hayes (pp. 212-222); "Femininity and Athleticism: Conflict or Consonance?" by Dorothy V. Harris (pp. 222-239); "Feminism, the Jockocracy, and Men's Liberation: Crying all the Way to the Bank" by Marjory Nelson (pp. 239-248); and "The Future of Women's Sport: Issues, Insights, and Struggles" by Bonnie A. Beck (pp. 299-314).

21   SCHREIBER, LINDA and STANG, JOANNE. *Marathon Mom*. Boston: Houghton Mifflin Co., 190 pp.
     Describes the introduction to running of a nonathletic mother of five; details the steps taken to achieve marathon distances. Includes training techniques, effects of running on the body, emotional benefits of running, and relationships between menstruation, pregnancy, and running.

22   SIEGEL, ALICE, and McLOONE, MARGO. *It's a Girl's Game, Too*. New York: Holt, Rinehart and Winston, 128 pp.
     Includes information about eighteen sports; gives a brief overview of the nature of the activity; the vocabulary of the game; necessary equipment; and where it can be played. Designed primarily as a means to encourage young girls to develop an interest in sports participation.

23   THACHER, ALIDA M. *Fastest Woman on Earth*. Milwaukee: Raintree Publishers, 45 pp.
     Follows career of Kitty O'Neil, who, though deaf, holds automobile land speed records, is a drag racer, and stunt woman.

24 _____. *Perilous Journey to the Top*. Milwaukee: Raintree Publishers, 47 pp.

Offers a brief account of the first successful attempt by American women to reach the summit of Annapurna in 1978.

25 ULLYOT, JOAN L. *Running Free*. New York: G.P. Putnam's Sons, 287 pp.

Could be described as the complete running book for women. Includes values of taking up the sport, psychological aspects of running, brief profiles of women runners older than thirty years (one in her eighties), and a section about Ullyot's own introduction to and experiences in running. A final section includes several instructional chapters covering training, medical issues, running apparel, and controversies and myths that surround the woman's running experience.

26 WARREN, WILLIAM E. *Zone Offenses for Women's Basketball*. Boston: Allyn & Bacon, 280 pp.

Focuses on the patterns and techniques when facing a zone defense on the court. Includes discussion of zone defense and drills for practicing offensive tactics against the defense.

27 WILEY, JACK. *Women's Gymnastics*. Mountain View, Calif.: Anderson World, 185 pp.

Gives a general overview of women's gymnastics and methods for learning and teaching the sport. Analyzes skills for each event; includes conditioning exercises and a brief description of rules for competition.

28 WRIGHT, GRAEME. *Olympic Greats*. London: Queen Anne Press, 159 pp.

Contains nineteen selections of what the author views as great moments from the Olympic Games. Highlights significant accomplishments of six women in the Games: Babe Didrikson in 1932; Fanny Blankers-Koen in 1948; Anita Lonsbrough in 1960; Mary Peters in 1972; Olga Korbut in 1972; and Nadia Comaneci in 1976.

29 WRIGHT, SHANNON, with KEELEY, STEVE. *The Women's Book of Racquetball*. Chicago: Contemporary Books, 238 pp.

Explains the game of racquetball and equipment needed for it. Analyzes the skills of the game; identifies common errors and suggested corrections. Features innumerable photographs illustrating the text.

1981

1   AESENG, NATHAN. *Winning Women of Tennis.* Minneapolis: Lerner Publishers Co., 80 pp.
    Contains brief biographical sketches and highlights of their professional careers for Helen Wills, Althea Gibson, Margaret Court, Billie Jean King, Chris Evert, Evonne Goolagong, Martina Navratilova, and Tracy Austin.

2   BACHTER, MARC; with HENDERSON, AMY; HUSSEY, JEANNETTE; and CHRISTMAN, MARGARET C.S. *Champions of American Sport.* New York: Harry N. Abrams, 288 pp.
    Presents brief biographical sketches of athletes selected for exhibition in the National Portrait Gallery of the Smithsonian Institution in 1981. Includes Patty Berg (p. 142), Helen Wills (p. 154), Billie Jean King (p. 164), Gertrude Ederle (p. 170), Sonja Henie (p. 180), Tenley Albright (p. 184), Peggy Fleming (p. 186), Babe Didrikson (p. 198), and Wilma Rudolph (p. 206).

3   BORMS, J.; HEBBELINCK, M.; and VENERANDO, A. *Women and Sport: An Historical, Biological, Physiological, and Sportsmedical Approach.* New York: Karger, 242 pp.
    Presents a collection of thirty-one selected papers from the International Congress on Women and Sport held in Rome in 1980. Topics cover the wide range of subject matter identified in the title.

4   BROOKS, CHRISTINE. *Women's Hurdling: Novice to Champion.* Champaign, Ill.: Leisure Press, 128 pp.
    Discusses the techniques of successful hurdling, including mechanics and their application in the event. Presents basic principles for training and suggestions for weight training.

5   CLARK, PATRICK. *Sports Firsts.* New York: Facts on File, 287 pp.

Outlines hundreds of "firsts" in the sport world, many of which involve women. Scattered throughout the book are examples such as the first woman baseball umpire, the first black woman jockey, the first woman coxswain of a men's varsity crew, the first major women's outdoor track and field meet, the first woman's boxing match in the United States, and the first woman to win the Sullivan Award. Includes a brief commentary for each "first" that is cited.

6 EMERT, PHYLLIS RAYBIN. *Jane Frederick: Pentathlon Champion*. New York: Harvey House Publishers, 64 pp.

Outlines Frederick's athletic career from her introduction to track as a seven-year-old through her competition in the Olympic trials in 1980 at age twenty-eight.

7 FIGLER, STEPHEN K. "Women in Sport: Sex Roles and Sexism." In *Sport and Play in American Life*. Philadelphia: W.B. Saunders Co., pp. 262-294.

Examines the sociological perspectives of the female in sport. Considers such topics as role conflict, patriarchy in sports, and androgyny as an alternative role. Discusses some of the strong leaders in the women's sports movement and the role of Title IX in effecting change.

8 FONDA, JANE. *Jane Fonda's Workout Book*. New York: Simon & Schuster, 254 pp.

Is a general conditioning and exercise book introduced with a personal profile of the author, explaining her interest in health and fitness. Includes beginning and advanced activities and exercises for special problems such as lower back pain and dysmenorrhea

9 FOX, MARY VIRGINIA. *The Skating Heidens*. Hillside, N.J.: Enslow Publishers, 127 pp.

Chronicles the racing experiences of speed skaters Beth and Eric Heiden, and their successes in the 1980 winter Olympics.

10 ____. *Janet Guthrie: Foot to the Floor*. Minneapolis: Dillon Press, 46 pp.

Traces the automobile racing career of Guthrie, who was the first woman driver to compete in the Indianapolis 500.

11 GREEN, TINA SLOAN; OGLESBY, CAROLE A.; ALEXANDER, ALPHA; and FRANKE, NIKKI. *Black Women in Sport*. Reston, Va.: American Alliance for Health, Physical Education, Recreation, and Dance, 80 pp.

Focuses on the involvement of black women in sport and the problems and prejudices they have faced. Includes brief biographical sketches of seventeen black women who have achieved success in the sports world.

12 HAHN, JAMES, and HAHN, LYNN. *Chris! The Sports Career of Chris Evert Lloyd*. Mankato, Minn.: Crestwood House, 41 pp.

Outlines Evert Lloyd's life and tennis career, highlighting her major competitions.

13 _____. *Patty! The Sports Career of Patricia Berg*. Mankato, Minn.: Crestwood House, 47 pp.

Presents biographical information for Patty Berg, the first person honored in the World Golf Hall of Fame. Includes her early life and the many achievements of her lengthy career.

14 _____. *King! The Sports Career of Billie Jean King*. Mankato, Minn.: Crestwood House, 47 pp.

Describes King's early family life; discusses her tennis career, both amateur and professional.

15 _____. *Zaharias! The Sports Career of Mildred Zaharias*. Mankato, Minn.: Crestwood House, 47 pp.

Offers a brief overview of the life and athletic career of Babe Didrikson Zaharias. Describes her early life in Beaumont, Texas and her athletic successes in basketball, track and field, and golf.

16 HULT, JOAN S., and PARK, ROBERTA J. "The Role of Women in Sports." In *Sports in Modern America*, edited by William J. Baker and John M. Carroll. St. Louis: River City Publishers, pp. 115-128.

Offers a brief, general description of sporting developments for women focusing primarily on activities of the twentieth century. Identifies several prominent athletes and their accomplishments and describes the efforts of women to achieve equality in sport in the 1960s and 1970s.

17   JONES, BETTY MILLSAPS. *Wonder Women of Sports*. New York: Random House, 69 pp.

Presents brief sketches of twelve athletes, focusing generally on a major feat or event that would warrant the title "wonder woman." Examples include Diana Nyad's sixty-mile swim; Kitty O'Neil's role as a Hollywood stunt woman; Roberta Bergay's entry as the first woman in the Boston marathon in 1966. Other athletes are Billie Jean King, Annie Peck, Nadia Comaneci, Mickey Wright, Wilma Rudolph, Joan Joyce, Babe Didrikson, Sonja Henie, and Althea Gibson.

18   KEESE, PARTON. "Billie Jean King A Sense of Urgency." In *The Measure of Greatness*. Englewood Cliffs, N.J.: Prentice-Hall, pp. 69-82.

Attempts to answer the question regarding sport, "What leads to greatness?" Focuses on King's tennis career and her major accomplishments as a player.

19   LYON, LISA, and HALL, DOUGLAS KENT. *Lisa Lyon's Body Magic*. New York: Bantam Books, 183 pp.

Discusses a bodybuilding program for women developed by Lyon, the first World Women's Bodybuilding champion, and ways to achieve personal goals in the activity. Includes vignettes of women throughout history who have been characterized as strong women,

20   MADISON, ARNOLD. *How to Play Girl's Softball*. New York: Julian Messner, 125 pp.

Discusses the history of softball, equipment and clothing for playing the game, and rules. Analyzes skills and playing techniques, including those for advanced play.

21 MARSHALL, JOHN L., with BARBASH, HEATHER. *The Sports Doctor's Fitness Book for Women*. New York: Delacorte Press, 383 pp.

Discusses the myths about women and sport and the physiological differences between women and men. Suggests training procedures to develop total fitness, activities for women over forty-five, and how to choose a sport to fit one's own fitness needs. Includes information on nutrition and care and prevention of injuries.

22 McDONALD, DAVID, and DREWERY, LAUREN. *Canada's Greatest Women Athletes*. New York: John Wiley and Sons, 274 pp.

Sketches briefly the athletic careers of thirty seven of Canada's top women athletes.

23 MYERS, GAIL ANDERSEN. *A World of Sport for Girls*. Philadelphia: The Westminster Press, 159 pp.

Explores athletic opportunities available to women and briefly highlights some of their sport successes. Discusses such topics as choosing a coach, getting an athletic scholarship, and available career opportunities other than teaching, coaching, and playing.

24 NYAD, DIANA, and HOGAN, CANDACE LYLE. *Diana Nyad's Basic Training for Women*. New York: Harmony Books, 191 pp.

Presents a basic training program for women designed to strengthen the body and improve the quality of life. Suggests pretraining conditioning for both mind and body; includes weight training activities and advanced training experiences. Offers hints on injury prevention, diet, and exercise during pregnancy.

25 PACHTER, MARC; HENDERSON, AMY; HUSSEY, JEANNETTE; and CHRISTMAN, MARGARET C.S., eds. *Champions of American Sport*. New York: Harry N. Abrams, 288 pp.

Presents brief, illustrated biographical texts for 100 well-known athletes. Women athletes included are Patty Berg (golf); Helen Wills, Billie Jean King (tennis); Gertrude Ederle (swimming); Tenley Albright, Peggy Fleming (ice skating); and Babe Didrikson, Wilma Rudolph (track).

26   SONS, RAY. *Andrea Jaeger: Pro in Ponytails*. Chicago: Children's Press, 46 pp.

Gives a brief overview of Jaeger's tennis career after turning professional at age fourteen.

27   STANEK, CAROLYN. *The Complete Guide to Women's College Athletics*. Chicago: Contemporary Books, 251 pp.

Written as a handbook for the female high school student who may be interested in participating in collegiate athletics. Includes practical information about the recruiting process; what to look for and what to ask when visiting a campus; how to assess summer sport camps; and resolving the conflict of academics versus athletics.

28   SULLIVAN, GEORGE S. *Better Field Hockey for Girls*. New York: Dodd, Mead & Co., 63 pp.

Focuses primarily on the skills of field hockey and how to execute them. Includes team strategy and a glossary of terms used in the game. Generously illustrated with photographs.

29   ____. *Better Track Events for Girls*. New York: Dodd, Mead & Co., 64 pp.

Covers all the running events for girls, including cross-country and distance running. Suggests techniques for improving performance in each event.

30   ____. *Superstars of Women's Track*. New York: Dodd, Mead & Co., 129 pp.

Briefly sketches the sports careers of six successful track athletes. Highlights some of the outstanding performances of Evelyn Ashford, Mary Decker, Madeline Manning, Julie Shea, Grete Waitz, and Candy Young.

31   WEIDER, BETTY, and WEIDER, JOE. *The Weider Book of Bodybuilding for Women*. Chicago: Contemporary Books, 129 pp.

Covers training techniques and exercise for developing a successful weight training program. Offers suggestions for achieving success in competition.

32   WEISER, MARJORIE P.K., and ARBEITER, JEAN S. "Games Women Play." In *Womanlist*. New York: Atheneum, pp. 401-425.
     Lists hundreds of women who have achieved success in sport in some way; includes a brief statement for each about her achievement.

1982

1   CONROY, MARY, and RITVO, EDWARD. *Every Woman Can: The Conroy Method to Safety, Security, and Self Defense*. New York: Grosset & Dunlap, 218 pp.
    Details basic rules for personal safety and avoiding potential danger. Suggests tactics for defending oneself and common items that may be used as weapons. Discusses rape and strategies for dealing with it.

2   DONOVAN, PETE. *Carol Johnston, the One-Armed Gymnast*. Chicago: Children's Press, 42 pp.
    Briefly sketches Johnston's career as a gymnast and the success she achieved in spite of her handicap.

3   DYER, K.F. *Challenging the Men: The Social Biology of Female Sporting Achievement*. New York: University of Queensland Press, 286 pp.
    Examines the biological, psychological, and cultural requirements to achieve successful athletic performance. Discusses several activities in which women participate including record performances in the sports. Concludes with a look at future expectations for women in sport.

4   FERRIGNO, CARLA. *For Women Only*. Chicago: Contemporary Books, 139 pp.
    Focuses on the development of physical fitness for women. Discusses nutrition, mental attitude, increasing energy, and the exercise factors uniquely concerned with women. Includes a section on often-asked questions about fitness and answers for them.

5   GUILIANI, DOROTHY A. *Complete Guide to Coaching Women's Basketball*. West Nyack, N.Y.: Parker Publishing Co., 216 pp.

Focuses on knowledge and techniques for becoming a successful coach of competitive teams. Practical hints for planning the season introduce the book, and the bulk of information thereafter discusses developing and refining offensive and defensive team play.

6   HALL, M. ANN, and RICHARDSON, DOROTHY A. *Fair Ball: Towards Sex Equality in Canadian Sport*. Ottowa: The Canadian Advisory Council on the Status of Women, 124 pp.

Examines the issue of equality in sport, what does it mean, does it exist, and ways to effect change. Provides a brief history of sport for women in Canada and discusses the myths that prevail about women in sport.

7   HOWELL, REET, ed. *Her Story in Sport: A Historical Anthology of Women in Sports*. West Point, N.Y.: Leisure Press, 612 pp.

Contains a collection of forty-two essays that explore the historical development of sport for women. Three sections focus on selected time periods: prior to 1860; from 1860 to 1920; and 1920 to 1982. The remaining sections include selections concerning sport for women in academic settings and articles that explore specific developments in selected sports such as basketball, baseball, rodeo, and tennis.

8   KASKIE, SHIRLI. *A Woman's Golf Game*. Chicago: Contemporary Books, 207 pp.

Designed as an instructional manual for learning the game of golf. Includes detailed skill analysis for strokes, suggestions for making special shots, and instructions for left-handed golfers.

9   KING, BILLIE JEAN, with DEFORD, FRANK. *The Autobiography of Billie Jean King*. New York: Granada Publishing, 214 pp.

Begins with King's explanation of her extramarital affair with another woman, apparently to dispel what she viewed as the inaccuracies surrounding that part of her life. Offers an inside view of the ups and downs in her career along with some of the underlying philosophy that has endeared her to some and angered others. Woven throughout the narrative are highlights of her professional tennis career.

10   LIEBERMAN, NANCY. *Basketball My Way*. New York: Charles Scribner's Sons, 193 pp.

Uses a personal narrative approach in providing analysis of basketball skills and strategy. Includes hints for improving game play and brief information about conditioning, nutrition, and injuries. A beginning chapter describes Lieberman's introduction to basketball and her subsequent successes in the game.

11   LINK, SHEILA. *Women's Guide to Outdoor Sports*. Tulsa: Winchester Press, 238 pp.

Includes information on archery, backpacking, boating, camping, canoeing, cross-country skiing, fishing, hiking, hunting, shooting, and use of a map and compass. Focuses primarily on instructional tips for each of the activities in order to enjoy them. Has a number of suggestions for selecting or altering equipment to fit the female body frame.

12   LLOYD, CHRIS EVERT, with AMDUR, NEIL. *Chrissie, My Own Story*. New York: Simon & Schuster, 238 pp.

Details Evert Lloyd's life in the tennis world from her personal perspective. Discusses many of the highlights of her competitive matches; concludes with a complete statistical record of her career through 1981.

13   MEYER, GLADYS E. *Softball for Girls and Women*. New York: Charles Scribner's Sons, 319 pp.

Focuses on the skills for playing softball; provides skill analysis, practice drills, and defensive and offensive play. Includes suggestions for training and conditioning and organizational procedures for softball programs.

14   RADLAUER, RUTH, and RADLAUER, ED. *Some Basics about Women's Basketball*. Chicago: Children's Press, 32 pp.

Describes the game of basketball in simple language, including only the information for a basic understanding of the game. Covers rules, techniques, and strategy.

15   ROSENZWEIG, SANDRA. *Sportfitness for Women*. New York: Harper & Row, 447 pp.

Presents a detailed analysis of training and conditioning techniques with specific information applicable to thirty-nine different sports. Discusses the relationship of menstruation and pregnancy to exercise; concludes with a section on diagnosis, treatment, and prevention of sports injuries.

16   SPILMAN, CAROL. *The Over 40 Women's Fitness Book*. West Point, N.Y.: Leisure Press, 320 pp.

Discusses a variety of approaches for developing fitness in the older woman. Includes information on dieting, relaxation, back problems, arthritis, running, and exercises for specific body parts.

17   SULLIVAN, GEORGE S. *Better Field Events for Girls*. New York: Dodd, Mead & Co., 63 pp.

Covers all field events for girls with suggestions for improving performance. Includes information on conditioning for the field events. Lists national high school records for each event.

1983

1   AUCHINCLOSS, EVA. *Women's Sports Foundation Fitness and Sports Resource Guide*. Palo Alto, Calif.: Women's Sports Publications, 144 pp.

Contains a potpourri of information concerning women's sports including such topics as fitness; nutrition and conditioning; career opportunities in sport; fund raising and publicity for women's sports teams; and a general overview of the Women's Sports Foundation, its history, funding, and long-range plans.

2   BARRILLEAUX, DORIS. *Forever Fit*. South Bend, Ind.: Icarus Press, 165 pp.

Provides instructions for general exercises to develop fitness with two special chapters devoted to exercises for infants to adolescents, and exercises during menstruation, pregnancy, and menopause. A final chapter focuses on the sport of bodybuilding with a brief description of some of the requirements for the sport.

3   BOUTELIER, MARY A., and SAN GIOVANNI, LUCINDA. *The Sporting Woman*. Champaign, Ill.: Human Kinetics, 306 pp.

Examines the role of women in sport from the historical, psychological, and social perspective. Analyzes women's involvement in sport within the context of major social institutions of family, education, mass media, and government and public policy. The book is written from a feminist viewpoint and focuses on theoretical as well as practical issues of women's sport experiences.

4   CHAFFEE, SUZY, and ADLER, BILL. *I Love New York Fitness Book*. New York: William Morrow & Co., 220 pp.

Develops an exercise program for women that fits the busy demands of city living. Includes a series of progressive exercises for various parts of the body and exercises that can be done anytime, anywhere.

5   COMBES, LAURA. *Winning Women's Bodybuilding*. Chicago: Contemporary Books, 183 pp.

Discusses basic fundamentals and intermediate techniques of bodybuilding for women and techniques for achieving success in competition. Includes suggestions for training, diet, and developing a positive mental attitude.

6   CRATTY, BRYANT J. "Women in Sport." In *Psychology in Contemporary Sport*. Englewood Cliffs, N.J.: Prentice-Hall, pp. 163-189.

Synthesizes current research on the psychology of women in sport focusing on the topics of motivation, personality, and biological rhythms. Concludes with a look to the future and a lengthy bibliography.

7   DARDEN, ELLINGTON. *The Nautilus Woman*. New York: Simon & Schuster, 190 pp.

Describes the use of the Nautilus exercise machines for shaping the body and developing an attractive physical appearance. Includes a question/answer section about common concerns women express.

8   GREENSPAN, EMILY. *Little Winners, Inside the World of the Child Sports Star*. Boston: Little, Brown & Co., 309 pp.
    Examines the lives and sports careers of children under the age of twenty who have achieved success in sports competition. Attempts to answer questions and concerns related to entering competition at an early age. Includes several female athletes who have competed in individual sports.

9   HAMILL, DOROTHY, with CLAIRMONT, ELVA. *Dorothy Hamill, On and Off the Ice*. New York: Alfred A. Knopf, 189 pp.
    Describes Hamill's development into one of the world's finest figure skaters. Carefully details many of her experiences in amateur competition.

10 HANEY, LYNN. *Skaters: Profile of a Pair*. New York: G.P. Putnam's Sons, 64 pp.
    Focuses on the training and competitive experiences of pairs figure skaters Amy Grossman and Robert Davenport. Relates the special problems of achieving success in pairs skating.

11 HAYDEN, SANDY; HALL, DAPHNE; and STUECK, PAT. *Women in Motion*. Boston: Beacon Press, 151 pp.
    Takes a philosophic point of view in attempting an inspirational kind of book to encourage women to maintain active lives. Discusses the pros and cons of health clubs, finding new challenges in wilderness activities, and the individual values of movement. Concludes with a personal statement by each author about the meaning of movement to her.

12 MROZEK, DONALD J. "From 'Swooning Damsel' to Sportswoman: The Role of Women as a Constituency in Sport." In *Sport and American Mentality, 1880-1910*. Knoxville: University of Tennessee Press, pp. 136-160.
    Details the changing role of women in sport at the turn of the century, focusing especially on the activities deemed appropriate for women and the role of women physical educators in the promotion of sport in this time period.

13   PETERSON, SUSAN L. *The Woman's Stretching Book*. Champaign, Ill.: Leisure Press, 112 pp.

Presents a collection of exercises for increasing flexibility in all parts of the body. Exercises are arranged by body part, from easiest to most difficult; each exercise is illustrated with a photograph.

14   POSTOW, BETSY C., ed. *Women, Philosophy, and Sport: A Collection of New Essays*. Metuchen, N.J.: The Scarecrow Press, 330 pp.

Contains sixteen essays by different authors that address, from a philosophical point of view, three major questions: What constitutes fairness to women and girls in sport? What is the proper role of competition in sports? and What can theory of education teach us about physical education for women? Each section is introduced by the editor with general comments and a brief analysis of each of the essays.

15   RADER, BENJAMIN G. "Blacks and Women Demand Equal Opportunity." In *American Sports: From the Age of Folk Games to the Age of the Spectators*. Englewood Cliffs, N.J.: Prentice-Hall, pp. 324-344.

Directs about half of the discussion in a chapter to the changing role of women in sport, focusing primarily on the 1960s and 1970s with some brief references to American sportswomen between 1920 and 1960.

16   ROSEN, TRIX. *Strong and Sexy: The New Body Beautiful*. New York: The Putnam Publishing Group, 143 pp.

Presents a photo collection of women bodybuilders with a brief biographical narrative for each.

17   WADE, PAUL, and DUFFY, TONY. *Winning Women*. New York: Times Books, 156 pp.

Contains a collection of action photographs depicting outstanding women athletes. Includes most of the activities in which women participate, ranging from basketball and golf to water skiing and windsurfing. A short narrative introduces each of the four sections, "The Revolution," "The Body," "The Stars," and "The Future."

18 WOLF, MICHAEL D. *Nautilus Fitness for Women*. Chicago: Contemporary Books, 191 pp.

Presents a physical fitness approach for women through use of Nautilus exercise machines in conjunction with aerobic exercises.

1984

1 ANDERSON, DAVE. *Shooting for the Gold: A Portrait of America's Olympic Athletes*. Ottawa, Ill.: Jameson Books, 144 pp.

Presents a photographic tribute to the athletes vying for positions for the 1984 Olympic Games and those who eventually competed in the Games. Except for twelve pages of narrative focusing briefly and primarily on individual athletes, the book is devoted exclusively to photographs, of which almost half are of women.

2 *Atalanta*. Los Angeles: Papier-Mache' Press, 84 pp.

Presents a collection of poetry and short fiction as a tribute to women's athletic achievements. Includes the work of nineteen authors.

3 AVERBUCH, GLORIA. *The Woman Runner*. New York: Simon & Schuster, 223 pp.

Focuses on all aspects of running from a woman's point of view. Includes sections on woman and her body, tips on successful competition, and interviews with women runners who have fared well in competition. Offers support and encouragement to women runners and a guarded prediction for what the future holds for them.

4 BURSTEIN, NANCY *The Executive Body* New York: Simon & Schuster, 223 pp.

Written as a fitness guide for the professional woman. Provides information for staying in shape when traveling, fitness activities during the work day, exercises "from bed to bath to getting dressed," and an intensive at-home conditioning program. An entire section of five chapters is devoted to nutrition, considering the lifestyle of the professional woman; another section of three chapters deals with ways of managing stress. Of interest to the traveling businesswoman who wants to stay in shape is a state-by-state listing of hotels and motels that offer exercise facilities.

5   CURRY, TIMOTHY J., and JIOBU, ROBERT M. "The Sportswoman, Today, Yesterday, and Tomorrow." In *Sports, A Social Perspective*. Englewood Cliffs, N.J.: Prentice-Hall, pp. 159-181.

   Examines the role of women in sport from several different viewpoints, including gender roles and stereotypes, socialization, the Olympic Games, and professional sport.

6   EDITORS OF *FIT* MAGAZINE. *Women's Bodybuilding Photo Book*. Mountain View, Calif.: Anderson World Books, 128 pp.

   Presents a collection of photographs of women bodybuilders in various poses. Includes a selection of pictures from competitive events.

7   HEIDENSTAM, OSCAR. *Body Beautiful*. New York: Arco Publishing, 104 pp.

   Designed as an exercise guide for general use. Discusses the importance of exercise; describes exercises done with and without apparatus, use of household objects for resistance exercises, and basic weight training. A brief section outlines exercises suitable for pregnancy and postchildbirth.

8   HENRY, BILL, and YEOMANS, PATRICIA HENRY. *An Approved History of the Olympic Games*. Sherman Oaks, Calif.: Alfred Publishing Co., 512pp.

   Presents a historical overview of the Ancient and Modern Olympic Games and a narrative description of each Olympiad from 1896 through 1984. Lists official results of both summer and winter Games. Information concerning women is found throughout the book.

9   JOHNSON, CONNIE PETERSON, with WRIGHT, MARGIE. *The Woman's Softball Book*. New York: Leisure Press, 207 pp.

   Focuses on fast-pitch softball primarily for coaches. Includes skill analysis, offensive strategy, and practice drills for players. Has a long list of common errors and corrections for them.

10 KOCH, SUSAN. *Body Dynamics, the Body Shape-Up Book for Women*. New York: Leisure Press, 160 pp.

Presents a training program at three levels, body toning, conditioning for sports, and bodybuilding. Includes suggestions for preparing for bodybuilding competition.

11   OLINEKOVA, GAYLE. *The Sensuality of Strength*. New York: Simon & Schuster, 111 pp.

Encourages women to lead active lives; includes instructions for various exercises and answers to questions frequently asked about exercise. Generously illustrated with photographs suggesting the sensuality of a strong body.

12   SANDS, BILL. *Coaching Women's Gymnastics*. Champaign, Ill.: Human Kinetics Publishers, 280 pp.

Focuses on guidelines and principles for developing a systematic approach to the coaching of gymnastics. Includes a section on coaching philosophy, followed by thorough discussions on developing the competitive program; tactical, technical, and psychological preparation of athletes; and conditioning and training.

13   SHEAFER, SILVIA ANNE. *Olympic Women, The Best in the World*. Mariposa, Calif.: Journal Publications, 118 pp.

Documents the successes of women in the winter and summer Olympic Games from 1900 to the Winter Games in Sarajevo in 1984. Includes the gold medalists for all events in which women participated and brief biographical sketches for many of them.

14   SMITH, ANN. *The Gifted Figure: Proportioning Exercises for Large Women*. Santa Barbara, Calif.: Capra Press, 95 pp.

Designed to encourage the larger woman to become active and ultimately reshape her body through exercise. Explains and illustrates a series of exercises for improving the figure.

15   TINKELMAN, MURRAY. *Cowgirl*. New York: Greenwillow Books, 30 pp.

Details a young barrel racer's experience in her first rodeo. Very brief narrative is illustrated with full-page photographs.

16 WADE, VIRGINIA, with RAFFERTY, JEAN. *Ladies of the Court: A Century of Women at Wimbledon*. New York: Atheneum, 192 pp.

Published on the 100th anniversary of women's entry in the Wimbledon tournament in 1884; presents an historical overview of the tournament, highlights of the winning matches, and biographical data for the winners. An excellent collection of photographs, beginning with the Watson sisters who played each other in the final match in 1884, enhances the historical value of the book.

17 WALLECHINSKY, DAVID. *The Complete Book of the Olympics*. New York: Penguin Books, 654 pp.

Provides a brief history of the Olympic Games. Presents vignettes of historical interest for many of the events; includes medal winners and records for all sports, both current and discontinued. Information about women is found throughout the book.

18 YOUNG, FAYE, and COFFEY, WAYNE. *Winning Basketball for Girls*. New York: Facts on File Publications, 153 pp.

Written in language directed toward the player; includes techniques for getting into shape, for developing individual skills, and analyzes offensive and defensive strategy for game play.

1985

1 ACOSTA, R. VIVIAN, and CARPENTER, LINDA JEAN. "The Status of Women in Intercollegiate Athletics – A Five-Year National Study." In *Sport and Higher Education*, edited by Donald Chu, Jeffrey O. Segrave, and Beverly Becker. Champaign, Ill.: Human Kinetics Publishers, pp. 327-334.

Presents research data from a five-year study (1977-1982) concerned with opportunities for women in intercollegiate athletic programs and teams coached by women. Offers a brief analysis of data and identifies three or four major conclusions that may be drawn from the results.

2 BERST, BARBARA J. *I Love Softball*. Seattle: National Lilac Publishing Co. 72 pp.

Written in the words of a young female player. Offers hints for practice and game play and suggestions for league play.

131

3   BRIDGES, JOHN. "Women's Professional Football and the Changing Role of the Woman Athlete." In *American Sport Culture*, edited by Wiley Lee Umphlett, pp. 143-158.

Examines the Ohio-based National Women's Football League, in existence since 1965, and the possible conflict between athletic competition and the feminine role of women as defined by society. Based on data from interviews with players in the League; focuses on their views of what such an experience means to them.

4   BURKE, KATY. *The Handbook for Non-Macho Sailors*. Newport, R.I.: Seven Seas Press, 223 pp.

Described as a "book for people with weak bodies and strong minds" (p. xi), although not necessarily for women only. Focuses on ways to make sailing easier and use the body most effectively. Offers useful ideas to women whose strength, on average, is less than that of men.

5   CAMARILLO, SHARON, with WITTE, RANDY. *Barrel Racing*. Colorado Springs: Western Horseman, 143 pp.

Discusses selecting and training the barrel horse, learning to negotiate the barrel racing pattern, and tips for competitive performance. Includes a summary of rules; is generously illustrated with photographs.

6   CARPENTER, LINDA JEAN. *Gymnastics for Girls and Women*. West Nyack, N.Y.: Parker Publishing Co., 215 pp.

Focuses on developing a beginning and intermediate program of gymnastics. Includes skill analysis, safety procedures, conditioning, mechanical principles applied to gymnastics, and evaluation procedures.

7   CARPENTER, LINDA JEAN, and ACOSTA, R. VIVIAN. "Women in Sport." In *Sport and Higher Education*, edited by Donald Chu, Jeffrey O. Segrave, and Beverly Becker. Champaign, Ill.: Human Kinetics Publishers, pp. 313-325.

Provides a brief overview of the historical development of sport for women in the United States since 1920, focusing primarily on organizational structures governing women's sports. Briefly discusses the impact of Title IX on women's sports.

8   HART, STAN. *Once a Champion: Legendary Tennis Stars Revisited.*
     New York: Dodd, Mead & Co., 463 pp.
        Presents a unique approach to biographies of early tennis
     greats, "a list of ex-champions with whom I would play tennis and then
     interview" (p. 3). Includes biographical information from their early
     tennis careers and interesting insights into their lives at the present
     time. Women in the list are Pauline Betz Addie (pp. 3-18), Althea
     Gibson (pp. 19-34), Sarah Palfrey (pp. 35-46), Shirley Fry Irvin (pp. 95-
     114), Gertrude "Gussie" Moran (pp. 193-206), Alice Marble (pp. 207-
     221), Louise Brough (pp. 317-339), and Margaret Osborne Dupont (pp.
     390-406). Only persons agreeing to personal contact with the author are
     included in the book.

9   JOSEY, MARTHA, and CLACK, LINDA. *Martha Josey's Running
     to Win.* Karnack, Tex.: Josey Enterprises, 238 pp.
        Focuses on the sport of barrel racing. Discusses selecting and
     training the horse, recognizing trouble signs on the horse, and practice
     techniques. Suggests ways for developing a winner, including the rider's
     mental attitude.

10   KEOGH, BARBARA K., and SMITH, CAROL E. *Personal Par: A
     Psychological System of Golf for Women.* Champaign, Ill.: Human
     Kinetics Publishers, 97 pp.
        Based on psychological principles for improving one's golf
     game; includes discussion of anxiety, motivation, and attention as
     influences on performance. Offers suggestions for practice on and off
     the course and criteria for selecting a pro for instruction.

11   KNUDSON, R.R. *Babe Didrikson: Athlete of the Century.* New York:
     Viking Penguin, 57 pp.
        Details Didrikson's athletic career with anecdotes and
     descriptive passages appealing to young readers.

12   LEDER, JANE MERSKY. *Martina Navratilova.* Mankato, Minn.:
     Crestwood House, 48 pp.
        Outlines Navratilova's tennis career, focusing primarily on the
     period after her move to the United States and her professional career
     since 1975.

13 LINDE, KAREN, and HOEHN, ROBERT G. *Girls' Softball: A Complete Guide for Players and Coaches*. West Nyack, N.Y.: Parker Publishing Co., 203 pp.

Focuses on coaching techniques for improving all phases of softball play. Includes practice drills, hints for position play, team strategy, and skill analysis for pitching, catching, and batting. Suggests activities for players during the off-season of the game.

14 LLOYD, CHRIS, and LLOYD, JOHN, with THATCHER, CAROL. *Lloyd on Lloyd*. New York: Beaufort Books, 215 pp.

Describes both the lives and tennis careers of each of the Lloyds; presents a chronology of their six years as husband and wife on the tennis circuit.

15 MARKEL, ROBERT, and MARKEL, NANCY BROOKS. *For the Record: Women in Sports*. New York: World Almanac Publishers, 204 pp.

Includes brief biographical sketches of women athletes in all sports from badminton to volleyball. Presents records and a list of champions for most sports.

16 *The Miller Lite Report on Women in Sports*. Iselin, N.J.: New World Decisions, 172 pp.

Reports results of a questionnaire sent to a random sample of 7,000 members of the Women's Sports Foundation. Focuses on the four general topics of sports interest, sports participation, spectator sports interest, and general opinion of women in sports. A copy of the questionnaire and a summary of results are included.

17 MITTELSTADT, MICHAL LOUISE. *Carefree Golf for Women*. San Gabriel, Calif.: Catalist Golf Publishing Co., 92 pp.

Written as a basic instructional text for the beginning golfer. Has a very brief section on skill development with more focus on selecting equipment, scoring, rules, course etiquette, and golf-type games. A cursory review of women's golf history is provided.

18 NAVRATILOVA, MARTINA, with VECSEY, GEORGE. *Martina*. New York: Alfred A. Knopf, 287 pp.

Details Navratilova's early life, growing up in Czechoslovakia, her first tennis experiences there, and her continuing success in the United States. Discusses her controversial relationships with well-known figures Rita Mae Brown, Nancy Lieberman, and Renée Richards. Focuses as much on her personal life as her tennis career.

19 POWERS, STEFANIE, and QUINE, JUDY. *Stefanie Powers: Superlife!* New York: Simon & Schuster, 223 pp.

Presents a physical fitness regime based on the philosophy and skills of the ancient discipline, karate.

20 REEDER, AMY L., and FULLER, JOHN R., eds. *Women in Sport: Sociological and Historical Perspectives*. Atlanta: Darby Printing Company, 77 pp.

Contains a collection of five essays representing diverse theoretical approaches to the study of women in sport. Subjects included are governance, athletic participation and academic achievement, allocation of resources (high school), the feminist perspective in sport, and English riding as a woman's sport.

21 RUST, ART, Jr., and RUST, EDNA. "Althea Gibson." In *Art Rust's Illustrated History of the Black Athlete*. Garden City, N.Y.: Doubleday & Co., pp. 407-413.

Provides biographical information about tennis champion Althea Gibson, her early life, and her success as the first black to play in the USLTA championship at Forest Hills.

22 SILVERSTEIN, HERMAN. *Mary Lou Retton and the New Gymnasts*. New York: Franklin Watts, 83 pp.

Describes the gymnastic styles and techniques of a group of women and men considered new to the sport with a major focus on Mary Lou Retton.

23 SIMON, ROBERT L. "Sex Equality in Sports." In *Sports and Social Values*. Englewood Cliffs, N.J.: Prentice-Hall, pp. 100-125.

Briefly examines the issues related to sex equality in sports including both the ideals of equality and providing for equivalent opportunities.

24 WASHINGTON, ROSEMARY G. *Mary Lou Retton, Power Gymnast.* Minneapolis: Lerner Publishing Co., 55 pp.
    Describes Retton's gymnastic career and training as she developed into the first American woman to win an Olympic gold medal in gymnastics.

25 WELLS, CHRISTINE L. *Sport & Performance: A Physiological Perspective.* Champaign, Ill.: Human Kinetics Publishers, 344 pp.
    Examines the physiological parameters of women's involvement in sport, specifically, adaptations to exercise, with information provided about both the young girl and the adult female. Includes sections on the menstrual function and exercise; the nonmenstruating woman, menopausal, postmenopausal, or pregnant; nutrition and weight control; and the high-level athlete.

1986

1 BELL, MARY M. "Role Conflict of Women as Athletes in the United States." In *Fractured Focus: Sport as a Reflection of Society* by Richard E. Lapchick. Lexington, Mass.: D.C. Heath & Co., pp. 139-149.
    Analyzes some of the research literature dealing with role conflict and female athletes.

2 BUCK, RAY. *Tiffany Chin: A Dream on Ice.* Chicago: Children's Press, 43 pp.
    Presents a brief biography of Chinese-American figure skater Tiffany Chin. Describes her various competitions including the 1984 Olympic Games.

3 COOK, JENNIFER, and WOLF, MICHAEL D. *Body Type Beautiful.* Chicago: Contemporary Books, 190 pp.
    Identifies four body types; offers exercises for improving each type. Includes a self-test for determining general fitness level and aerobic exercises for all body types. Concludes with a section on nutrition and the use of clothes to enhance the illusion of shape until the desired goal is reached through exercise.

4   DAY, ELIZABETH, and DAY, KEN. *Sports Fitness for Women*. London: B. T. Batsford, Ltd., 96 pp.

Focuses on conditioning and training exercises for developing a fitness level for sports participation. Includes instructions for performing the exercises, information about female physiology, and treatment for common injuries.

5   DRINKWATER, BARBARA L., ed. *Female Endurance Athletes*. Champaign, Ill.: Human Kinetics Publishers, 176 pp.

Focuses on diverse aspects of women's long-distance running. An historical overview of women's quest for opportunities in distance running is followed by discussions of psychology, biomechanics, nutrition, heat tolerance, amenorrhea, and injuries. Each topic is examined in relation to the effects of women's participation in distance running.

6   GREEN, HARVEY. *Fit for America*. New York: Pantheon Books, 367 pp.

Primarily concerned with general problems and changes in health and fitness in the United States from 1830 to 1940. Includes a significant amount of discussion throughout pertaining to women. Covers such topics as bicycling, dress reform, and exercises and sports for women.

7   HEMERY, DAVID. *The Pursuit of Sporting Excellence, a Study of Sport's Highest Achievers*. Champaign, Ill.: Human Kinetics Books, 295 pp.

Explores the factors that contribute to athletic excellence, physical, social, psychological, and moral. Profiles several athletes who have achieved success, twelve of them women. Includes career highlights and the athlete's view of her most memorable event or win for Ann Brightwell, Margaret Court, Shirley Strickland de la Hunty, Lucinda Palmer Green, Shane Gould Innes, Billie Jean King, Chris Evert Lloyd, Heather McKay, Marjorie Nelson, Joan Benoit Samuelson, Jayne Torvill, and Mary Rand Twomey.

8   JENSEN, JUDY. "Women's Collegiate Athletics: Incidents in the Struggle for Influence and Control." In *Fractured Focus: Sport as a*

Reflection of Society by Richard E. Lapchick. Lexington, Mass.: D.C. Heath & Co., pp. 151-161.

Examines the evolution of governance in women's collegiate sports leading to the establishment of the Association of Intercollegiate Athletics for Women.

9   KNUDSON, R.R. *Martina Navratilova, Tennis Power*. New York: Viking Penguin, 57 pp.

Contains biographical information about Navratilova's life and tennis career from her introduction to the game in her native country, Czechoslovakia, through her professional career in the United States.

10   LAGESE, JANE, and RUBENSTEIN, HELGE. *Fitness over 40: A Woman's Guide to Exercise, Health, and Emotional Wellbeing*. New York: Pantheon Books, 127 pp.

Focuses on the values of exercise for the woman over forty; discusses specific exercise-related problems, the stress of changing relationships after forty, and the importance of taking care of oneself. Includes specific exercises for various body parts and suggested daily and weekly exercise programs.

11   LASCO, DIANA. *Developing a Successful Women's Track and Field Program*. West Nyack, N.Y.: Parker Publishing Co., 227 pp.

Offers a practical guide for organizing a track and field program and the techniques and methods for coaching athletes. Covers the topics of drills and coaching tips for all events; includes practical tips for calendar planning, identifying potential champions, delegating responsibilities to gain more coaching time, injury prevention, and recruiting athletes.

12   LENSKYJ, HELEN. *Out of Bounds: Women, Sport and Sexuality*. Toronto: The Women's Press, 179 pp.

Explores the historical relationship between sport, femininity, and sexuality in North America, particularly Canada and the United States. Examines the issue of constraints on women in sport as a result of masculine control over female sexuality.

13 LOPIANO, DONNA A. "A Political Analysis of the Possibility of Impact Alternatives for the Accomplishment of Feminist Objectives within American College Sport." In *Fractured Focus: Sport as a Reflection of Society* by Richard E. Lapchick. Lexington, Mass.: D.C. Heath & Co., pp. 163-176.

    Focuses on the role of women in intercollegiate athletics and, more specifically, their future role in the NCAA, now the governing body for women's collegiate sport.

14 MARTZ, SANDRA, ed. *More Golden Apples*. Manhattan Beach, Calif.: Papier-Maché Press, 56 pp.

    Includes a collection of poetry and short fiction celebrating women's athletic accomplishments. All items are authored by women.

15 NEWMAN, MATTHEW. *Lynette Woodard*. Mankato, Minn.: Crestwood House, 48 pp.

    Follows the life and career of the first female to play basketball with the Harlem Globetrotters.

16 ____. *Mary Decker Slaney*. Mankato, Minn.: Crestwood House, 48 pp.

    Follows the champion runner from her first race at age eleven to championship performances as one of the top runners of the world.

17 NIELSEN, NICKI J. *The Iditarod: Women on the Trail*. Anchorage: Wolfdog Publishers, 73 pp.

    Presents the historical background of the Iditarod Trail and sled dog races along the Trail. Includes biographical profiles of the twenty-nine women who have entered the races from 1974 through 1985.

18 PEISS, KATHY. *Cheap Amusements: Working Women and Leisure in Turn-of-the-Century New York*. Philadelphia: Temple University Press, 255 pp.

    Describes the lives and culture of young working women in New York City between 1880 and 1920. Explores cultural changes in the lives of working women and examines the redefinition of gender relations occurring during the period by "focusing on the role of young white working women in fostering these changes" (p. 7). Concludes with case studies that focus on the commercialization of working class amusements, dance halls and amusement parks, for example.

19   PORTUGUES, GLADYS, and VEDRAL, JOYCE. *Hard Bodies*. New York: Dell Publishing Co., 203 pp.

Explains and illustrates a variety of bodybuilding exercises. Includes information on diet and exercise for specific body problem areas.

20   PUHL, JACQUELINE, and BROWN, C. HARMON. *The Menstrual Cycle and Physical Activity*. Champaign, Ill.: Human Kinetics Publishers, 174 pp.

Presents a collection of papers from a seminar at the Olympic Training Center, Colorado Springs, Colorado, in February, 1984. Includes a variety of topics such as amenorrhea, menstruation, and athletic performance; altered reproductive function and osteoporosis; and methodological problems in research on the menstrual cycle and physical activity.

21   RETTON, MARY LOU, and KAROLYI, BELA. *Mary Lou: Creating a Champion*. New York: McGraw-Hill Co., 189 pp.

Written in first person and alternating between narrative by Retton and Karolyi; relates Retton's development as a champion gymnast through her eyes and the eyes of her coach, Karolyi.

22   ROSENTHAL, BERT. *Lynette Woodard, The First Female Globetrotter*. Chicago: Children's Press, 43 pp.

Traces the career of basketball star Woodard, who made history when she joined the Harlem Globetrotters basketball team in 1986.

23   SOUTHALL, MARY, and BARTLETT, E.G. *Weight Training for Women*. North Pomfret, Vt.: David & Charles, 96 pp.

Explains and illustrates weight training activities as a part of fitness training. Includes advice on diet, relaxation, and basic equipment needed for the activities. Provides suggested training schedules to achieve selected goals.

24 SPEARS, BETTY. *Leading the Way: Amy Morris Homans and the Beginnings of Professional Physical Education for Women.* New York: Greenwood Press, 193 pp.

Details Homans' work in establishing one of the earliest physical education teacher training schools in the United States. Documents "her struggles to gain the acceptance of physical education as a profession for women and her unique approach to educating women in that profession" (p. 7). Focuses primarily on her work in the development of teacher training rather than her personal biography.

25 TOKARZ, KAREN. *Women, Sports, and the Law.* Buffalo, N.Y.: William S. Hein Co., 140 pp.

Provides a comprehensive annotated bibliography on women in sport, focusing primarily on legal issues and sex discrimination. Includes books, articles, cases, and statutes concerning sex discrimination as well as some selections with a sociological, psychological, or historical perspective.

26 VEDRAL, JOYCE. *Now or Never.* New York: Warner Books, 254 pp.

Presents a physical fitness program for women designed to offset the aging process. Includes activities for a workout at home or at a gym. Offers suggestions for diet and ways of motivating oneself to maintain a fitness program.

27 WEIDER, BEN, and KENNEDY, ROBERT. *Superpump! Hardcore Women's Bodybuilding.* New York: Sterling Publishing Co., 192 pp.

Presents brief biographical sketches of eighteen female bodybuilders. Includes comments about how their interest developed in the sport, some of their tips for success, and the training regime they follow.

1987

1 ADRIAN, MARLENE J. *Sportswomen: Medicine and Sport Science.* New York: Karger, 157 pp.

Contains a collection of research papers focusing on biological and sociopsychological factors that affect the role of sport in women's lives. Includes such topics as legal theory and sex discrimination; leisure

141

activities in ancient Greece and Rome; physical characteristics of young sportswomen; and the female breast in sports and exercise.

2   BENOIT, JOAN, with BAKER, SALLY. *Running Tide*. New York: Alfred A. Knopf, 213 pp.

Presents a personal testimony of the life and running career of marathoner Joan Benoit. Describes her interest in both field hockey and competitive skiing and her eventual primary focus on running. Details a number of the competitive events she has entered. Discusses other well-known women runners and pays tribute to those who paved the way for Benoit and others.

3   BLUE, ADRIANNE. *Grace Under Pressure: The Emergence of Women in Sport*. London: Sidgwick & Jackson, 228 pp.

Described as "an informal social history of the emergence of women in sport and an analysis of the state of play" (p. xiv). Identifies sport successes of several well-known athletes and includes information about some activities in which women have only recently become involved such as body building, weight lifting, and judo. Also includes information on drug use among women athletes and sex testing.

4   BULLARD, JIM. *Looking Forward to Being Attacked: Self-Protection for Every Woman*. New York: M. Evans & Co., 127 pp.

Focuses on learning to control fear and being prepared for attack if it should happen. Describes techniques for defending oneself from attack, dealing with obscene phone calls or peeping toms, and walking the streets safely.

5   CAIGNON, DENISE, and GROVES, GAIL. *Her Wits about Her: Self-Defense Success Stories by Women*. New York: Harper & Row, 347 pp.

Details the personal stories of some fifty women who resisted personal attacks and were, for the most part, successful in getting away or protecting themselves. Suggests ways of learning self-defense techniques.

6   GRIMSLEY, WILL. *101 Greatest Athletes of the Century*. New York: Bonanza Books, 320 pp.

Presents a well-illustrated description of the following twentieth-century female athletes: Nadia Comaneci, Margaret Court, Chris Evert, Sonja Henie, Billie Jean King, Suzanne Lenglen, Helen Wills Moody, Martina Navratilova, Wilma Rudolph, and Babe Didrikson Zaharias.

7   LOPEZ, NANCY, with WADE, DON. *Nancy Lopez's The Complete Golfer*. Chicago: Contemporary Books, 228 pp.

Written after Lopez's tenth year on the Ladies Professional Golf Association tour; reflects her wide range of experiences as a pro golfer. Analyzes the mechanics of the game and techniques for playing various shots. Offers advice for improving those skills. Includes sections on teaching children to play and exercise and nutrition for the golfer. Scattered throughout the book are brief biographical sketches of other successful women golfers.

8   MECHIKOFF, ROBERT A., and EVANS, VIRGINIA. *Sport Psychology for Women*. New York: Harper and Row, 202 pp.

Designed as a "learning tool and resource guide for coaches working with women athletes" (p. xiv). Discusses sociology and psychology of women athletes, aspects of motivation, and performance tools and techniques of applied sport psychology. The last half of the book focuses on applied psychological coaching methods derived from successful coaches in basketball, field hockey, gymnastics, softball, swimming, tennis, track and field, cross country, long-distance running, and volleyball. A brief profile of each coach is presented, followed by his/her psychological methods.

9   MORRISSEY, MURIEL, and OSBORNE, CAROL. *Amelia, My Courageous Sister*. Santa Clara, Calif.: Osborne Publishers, 312 pp.

Details Earhart's life and career through the eyes of her sister, Muriel. Includes a number of reproductions of letters and newspaper stories related to her life in aviation.

10   SHOEBRIDGE, MICHELE. *Women in Sport: A Select Bibliography*. New York: Mansell Publishing, 242 pp.

Includes bibliographical citations from the revival of the modern Olympics in 1896 up to the present, ranging from monographs and conference proceedings to theses, journal articles, and books.

Covers a broad range of subject areas including such topics as sociological and physiological aspects; the disabled; ethnic groups; the aged; sports equipment; sports medicine; and comparative sport.

11 SHRIVER, PAM; DeFORD, FRANK; and ADAMS, SUSAN B. *Passing Shots: Pam Shriver on Tour.* New York: McGraw-Hill Publishing Co., 223 pp.

    Written in diary form; describes, in her own words, a year in Shriver's life and tennis career. Includes her experiences on the tennis circuit from December 1984 to December 1985.

12 SMITH, KATHY, with JONES, JUDY. *Kathy Smith's Winning Workout.* Philadelphia: Running Press, 159 pp.

    Presents a twelve-week exercise program using free weights as a fast, effective means of getting in shape. Offers ideas for motivation and diet control.

1988

1 BEAZLEY, WILLIAM H., and HOBBS, JOSEPH H. "'Nice Girls Don't Sweat': Women in American Sport." In *The Sporting Image: Readings in American Sport History,* edited by Paul J. Zingg. New York: University Press of America, pp. 337-352.

    Briefly outlines some of the developments in women's sports opportunities in the twentieth century and the criticism that often accompanied their involvement.

2 BLUE, ADRIANNE. *Faster, Higher, Further: Women's Triumphs and Disasters at the Olympics.* London: Virago Press, 192 pp.

    Written primarily for the lay reader, includes a number of human interest stories about women's successes in the Olympic Games. Concludes with the records of all first-place women winners since 1900 when women participated in exhibition events in tennis and golf.

3 BULGER, MARGERY A. "American Sportswomen in the Nineteenth Century." In *The Sporting Image: Readings in American Sport History,* edited by Paul J. Zingg. New York: University Press of America, pp. 85-106.

Traces the sporting activities of nineteenth-century American women, their expanding opportunities after the Civil War, and their changing leisure habits as the century came to a close.

4   DUDEN, JANE. *Shirley Muldowney*. Mankato, Minn.: Crestwood House, 48 pp.

Presents a brief biography of drag racer Shirley Muldowney, the first person to win the Top Fuel Championship more than once.

5   ENGELMANN, LARRY. *The Goddess and the American Girl: The Story of Suzanne Lenglen and Helen Wills*. New York: Oxford University Press, 478 pp.

Offers a lengthy treatise on the lives and tennis careers of two of the greatest players in the 1920s and 1930s. Is probably the most definitive biographical treatment of the two individuals whose outstanding careers have received limited attention in prior years. Long, separate chapters are devoted to the life of each woman; following chapters detail many of the tennis activities in which the two women competed.

6   GUTTMANN, ALLEN. "Women's Sports," in *A Whole New Ball Game*. Chapel Hill: The University of North Carolina Press, pp. 139-158.

Presents a brief overview of selected aspects of the historical development of women's sports, with a major portion of the essay focusing on the 1970s.

7   HUGMAN, BARRY J., and ARNOLD, PETER. *The Olympic Games: Complete Track and Field Results, 1896-1988*. New York: Facts on File, 384 pp.

Lists all women competitors since their entry in Olympic track and field in 1928, with their event, place, time or distance, and medal won, if any. Includes a narrative account of the highlights at each Olympiad and brief biographical sketches of some of the top performers.

8   KNUDSON, R.R. *Julie Brown, Racing Against the World*. New York: Viking Penguin, 55 pp.

Briefly recounts the running career of Julie Brown, one of the United States runners in the first women's Olympic marathon in 1984.

9   LYNN, ELIZABETH A. *Babe Didrikson Zaharias*. New York: Chelsea House Publishers, 111 pp.

Chronicles Didrikson's life and athletic career from amateur to professional status. Relates her involvement with a number of sports other than track and golf in which she achieved championship status. Presents a chronological outline of her life.

10 MARIOLLE, ELAINE, and SHERMER, MICHAEL. *The Woman Cyclist*. Chicago: Contemporary Books, 393 pp.

Presents materials on touring and recreational cycling, mountain biking, competitive cycling, and endurance cycling. Includes training techniques, mechanical information for becoming self-sufficient on the road, and guidelines for selecting bikes and equipment. Details Mariolle's experiences in her three Race Across America competitions.

11 McCRONE, KATHLEEN E. *Playing the Game*. Lexington: University Press of Kentucky, 310 pp.

Details the historical development of women's sport in England between 1870 and 1914. Focuses on the "riding middle ranks" (preface) and fails to mention sport among the working class, a deliberate choice by the author. Topics include sport at Oxbridge Women's College and in the Public Schools; the medical and scientific debate about women's sport; sport and dress reform; and the literature of women's sport.

12 MONROE, JUDY. *Steffi Graf*. Mankato, Minn.: Crestwood House, 48 pp.

Briefly details Graf's tennis career, including her first Grand Slam Tournament win at the age of seventeen.

13 MORGAN, WILLIAM J., and MEIER, KLAUS V., eds. "Women and Sport." In *Philosophic Inquiry in Sport*. Champaign, Ill.: Human Kinetic Publishers, pp. 329-373.

Presents five essays focusing on women in sport under the larger subject heading, "Sport and Ethics." Includes "Sex Equality in Sports" by Jane English, "The Exclusion of Women from Sport: Conceptual and Existential Dimensions" by Iris Marion Young, "Women, Sex, and Sports" by Raymond A. Belliotti, "Human Equality in Sports" by Peter S. Wenz, and "Women and Masculine Sports" by Betsy Postow.

14   OVERTON, TED. "Women in Sport." In *Sports after Fifty*. Annapolis, Md.: Azimuth Press, pp. 167-172.
Focuses on ways of getting the woman over fifty involved in activity, especially if she has not been a sports participant in prior years.

15   PEARLMAN, BARBARA. *Workouts that Work for Women Who Work*. New York: Doubleday, 202 pp.
Presents a collection of exercises for the busy woman that may be performed without special equipment or facilities.

16   PORTER, DAVID L., ed. *Biographical Dictionary of American Sports, Outdoor Sports*. New York: Greenwood Press, 748 pp.
Provides brief biographies of seventy-five women who have excelled in a variety of outdoor sports from the early 1900s to the present. Arranged alphabetically by sport, entries include personal data and information about the person's sport career.

17   PUHL, JACQUELINE; BROWN, C. HARMON; and VOY, ROBERT O., eds. *Sport Science Perspectives for Women*. Champaign, Ill.: Human Kinetics Books, 248 pp.
Presents a collection of research papers from a conference held at the Olympic Training Center, Colorado Springs, Colorado, in 1985 that focused on information useful in planning training programs for women athletes. Selected topics include biomechanics, conditioning and rehabilitation, ergogenic aids, pregnancy and exercise, nutrition, eating disorders, stress, and motivation.

18   SHANGOLD, MONA M., and MIRKIN, GABE, eds. *Women and Exercise: Physiology and Sports Medicine*. Philadelphia: F.A. Davis Co., 299 pp.

Presents a collection of research-based papers focusing on health maintenance, injury treatment, and rehabilitation for women who exercise. Includes information on training, pregnancy, menstruation, and eating disorders.

19 STEWART-ROACHE, CATHARINE, and HARRISON-DAVIS, MARVEL. *Attractive Woman, A Physical Fitness Approach to Emotional and Spiritual Well-Being.* Albuquerque: Hermosa Publishers, 191 pp.

Focuses on the linkage between mental health and a physically active lifestyle. Discusses goal setting, diet, and dealing with stress and emotional highs and lows. Includes a variety of activity choices for exercising.

20 SULLIVAN, GEORGE S. *Great Lives: Sports.* New York: Macmillan Publishing Co., 285 pp.

Profiles the lives and sports careers of individuals who were the best in their sport or who had a major impact on their sport. Provides a brief career overview for Nadia Comaneci (pp. 60-69), Peggy Fleming (pp. 90-98), Babe Didrikson (pp. 70-79), Billie Jean King (pp. 143-149), and Martina Navratilova (pp. 168-177).

21 VERBRUGGE, MARTHA H. *Able-Bodied Womanhood.* New York: Oxford University Press, 305 pp.

Focuses on the relationships between health, fitness, and femininity between 1830 and 1900. Drawing from the study of three Boston institutions concerned with middle class women's health and exercise, the author presents an analysis of the "relationship between personal health and social change in nineteenth-century Boston" (p. 10). Includes numerous historical notes and a lengthy bibliography.

22 WILLIAMSON, TONI. *Twenty Names in Sport.* New York: Marshall Cavendish, 48 pp.

Sketches the highlights of the athletic careers of Babe Didrikson (pp. 12-13), Dawn Fraser (pp. 22-23), Billie Jean King (pp. 332-33), Olga Korbut (pp. 38-39), and Martina Navratilova (pp. 40-41).

23 ZIPTER, YVONNE. *Diamonds are a Dyke's Best Friend*. Ithaca, N.Y.: Firebrand Books, 223 pp.

Examines the "special relationship between lesbians and softball" (p. 18) and its role in the lesbian community. Includes a brief overview of American women in sport and a number of personal statements by women for whom softball has a special importance. Offers suggestions for improving sports opportunities for women in the future.

1989

1 BAILEY, COVERT, and BISHOP, LEA. *The Fit-or-Fat Woman*. Boston: Houghton Mifflin Co., 159 pp.

Examines the differences between women and men concerning body weight; discusses physiological aspects of weight gain and an exercise regime for lowering weight and developing physical fitness.

2 BIRACREE, TOM. *Althea Gibson*. New York: Chelsea House Publishers, 109 pp.

Follows the life and tennis career of Althea Gibson, the first black woman to win at Wimbledon.

3 FRANCIS, BEV, with REYNOLDS, BILL. *Bev Francis' Power Bodybuilding*. New York: Sterling Publishing Co., 160 pp.

Presents the basic techniques of bodybuilding, training procedures, diet, and care of injuries. Offers hints for achieving success in bodybuilding at the competitive level.

4 LAY, NANCY E. *The Summitt Season*. Champaign, Ill.: Leisure Press, 156 pp.

Chronicles the 1987-88 season of the 1987 NCAA basketball champions, the Lady Vols (Volunteers), and their efforts to repeat the national championship. Provides biographical information about the Vols' coach, Pat Head Summitt, and a considerable amount of insight into the interrelationships between a coach and her team.

5 LEVINE, ELLEN. *Ready, Aim, Fire! The Real Adventures of Annie Oakley*. New York: Scholastic, 132 pp.

Chronicles the life of Annie Oakley, who learned her skills as a sharpshooter by shooting game to help feed her family when women were expected to stay in the home. Describes her life as a performer in wild west shows until her retirement after a train accident.

6   LEVINE, PETER. "Women and Sport." In *American Sport: A Documentary History*. Englewood Cliffs, N.J.: Prentice Hall, pp. 160-193.

Focuses on twentieth-century sport; presents excerpts from primary documents written about basketball in 1913, sport philosophy in 1969, Billie Jean King in 1974, and Title IX in 1979. Illustrates both progress and problems confronted by women in the athletic realm.

7   LOVELL, MARY S. *The Sound of Wings: The Life of Amelia Earhart*. New York: St. Martin's Press, 445 pp.

Presents a detailed biography of Amelia Earhart, focusing to a great extent on her life with her husband, George Putnam. Attempts to clarify Putnam's role in Earhart's professional career in aviation.

8   LYNN, ELIZABETH A. *Babe Didrikson Zaharias's*. New York: Chelsea House Publishers, 111 pp.

Describes Zaharias' athletic career and the versatile accomplishments achieved in her short lifetime. A number of excellent photographs not generally found in other biographies provide unusual insight into the many faces of Babe Didrikson Zaharias.

9   PORTER, DAVID L., ed. *Biographical Dictionary of American Sports, Indoor Sports*. New York: Greenwood Press, 826 pp.

Provides brief biographies of more than sixty women who have excelled in a variety of indoor sports from the early 1900s to the present. Arranged alphabetically by sport, entries include personal data and information about each person's sports career.

10   RIDDLES, LIBBY, and JONES, TIM. *Race Across Alaska: First Woman to Win the Iditarod Tells Her Story*. Harrisburg, Pa.: Stackpole Books, 239 pp.

Chronicles Riddles' eighteen-day trek across Alaska in 1985 when she became the first woman to win the Iditarod Race. Gives a day-by-day account of the trip in diary form. Several informative narratives about dog racing, rules of the Iditarod Race, and description of the Trail are interspersed throughout the book.

11   SEIBERT, DAVID B., ed. *The Lincoln Library of Sports Champions*. Columbus, Ohio: Frontier Press Co., 20 vols., 127 pp. ea.

Contains brief biographies of successful athletes in a variety of sports. Arranged in alphabetical order, by volume, women are found throughout the collection. Volume twenty provides an index for the entire collection. Selection was based on the significance of the athlete and contributions to her sport. Emphasizes contemporary athletes such as Jackie Joyner-Kersee, though several earlier stars such as Helen Wills and Babe Didrikson are included. Generously illustrated with photographs.

12   SPARHAWK, RUTH M.; LESLIE, MARY E.; TURBOW, PHYLLIS; and ROSE, ZINA, *American Women in Sport, 1887-1987*, Metuchen, N.J.: The Scarecrow Press, 165 pp.

Presents a year-by-year chronology of the important milestones for women in sport; lists major individual achievements by women in sport over the past century.

13   TAMES, RICHARD. *Amelia Earhart*. New York: Franklin Watts, 32 pp.

Briefly traces Earhart's life and career as a pilot until her disappearance in 1937.

1990

1   COAKLEY, JAY J. "Gender Relations, Are the Barriers for Girls and Women Gone?" in *Sport and Society: Issues and Controversies*, 4th ed. St. Louis: Times Mirror/Mosby College Publishing, pp. 176-202.

Focuses on the increasing opportunities for women in sport and the reasons for such changes. Identifies forms of discrimination that continue to exist and suggests some political and organizational issues that still need to be addressed.

2 ROBERTSON, JANET. *The Magnificent Mountain Women*. Lincoln: University of Nebraska Press, 237 pp.

Recounts the exploits of mountain women in the Colorado Rocky Mountains. Includes mountain climbers and other recreational mountaineers as well as women who earned their livelihood in the mountains.

Chapter 5

Other Sources of Information

As women's sports programs have developed and participation by women has grown, acceptance of the athletic female has also increased. Sporting opportunities are currently available at all levels of participation for the interested woman. Periodicals devoted exclusively to women's sports interests are published, and many other sport magazines have increased the coverage devoted to women's concerns.

Concurrent with these developments has been greater recognition for the woman in sport. Induction into a sport hall of fame has been a traditional means of honoring outstanding athletes. Some halls of fame have been established exclusively for women. Others include women along with men; the number of male inductees, however, still far outweighs the number of females. With such a landmark decision as the recognition of the All American Professional Girls' Baseball League and women owners and umpires by the Baseball Hall of Fame in Cooperstown, New York, some of the last barricades may be falling.

Although many sources of information have been unconcerned with sports for women until fairly recently, the sports organization is an exception. Many women's sports organizations have been in existence for quite some time, and many mixed-sex organizations have included women from the date they were established. The promotion of sport for women has been enhanced by these groups, and opportunities have been provided that might otherwise have been a long time in coming. Perhaps the decade of the nineties will become known as the "Golden Age of Sport for Women."

Periodicals

American Fencing, 1949. 1750 E. Boulder St., Boulder, CO 80909.
Features articles of interest to the competitive fencer; publishes information concerning international competition.

American Fitness, 1983. 15250 Ventura Blvd., Suite 310, Sherman Oaks, CA 91403.
Focuses on health and fitness activities including nutrition, travel, sports, and motivation.

American Rowing, 1969. United States Rowing Association, 201 South Capitol Ave., No. 400, Indianapolis, IN 46225-1054.
Covers both recreational and competitive rowing; includes information on technique, regatta results, and individual profiles.

American Woman Road Rider, 1989. Box 536, Santa Monica, CA 90406.
Provides information for women riders of all kinds of motorcycles.

Athletic Training, 1956. National Athletic Trainers Association, Inc., Box 600, Winterville, NC 28590.
Focuses on sports medicine information including prevention and treatment of sports injuries.

Back to Health Magazine, 1988. Technologies, Inc., 1761 W. Hillsboro Blvd., Suite 203, Deerfield Beach, FL 33442-9920.
Focuses on back pain with suggestions for pain relief, diet, and mental health.

Badminton USA, 1967. United States Badminton Association, P.O. Box 456, Waterford, MI 48095.
Publishes results of competition; features articles on national and local badminton activities.

Balls and Strikes, 1933. 2801 Northeast 50th St., Oklahoma City, OK 73111.
Features general information on the sport of softball.

Bicycle USA, 1965. League of American Wheelmen, 6707 Whitestone Rd., Suite 209, Baltimore, MD 21207.
Provides information about touring, equipment, and club activities; covers various other cycling topics.

Bicycling, 1962. Rodale Press, Inc., 33 E. Minor St., Emmaus, PA 18049.

Features fitness activities for cycling; includes bike repair, travel and touring information, and bicycle racing.

Coaching Volleyball, 1987. Human Kinetics Publishers, P.O. Box 5076, Champaign, IL 61820.
Features information on techniques, strategy, sports medicine, and research findings. Profiles successful coaches.

Coaching Women's Basketball, 1987. Human Kinetics Publishers, Box 5076, Champaign, IL 61820.
Features articles on coaching techniques, recruiting, injuries, training, and conditioning.

Cycling U.S.A.. 1750 E. Boulder St., Colorado Springs, CO 80909.
Official publication of the United States Cycling Federation; features information on bicycle racing.

Eagle, 1932. United States Field Hockey Association, Inc., 1750 East Boulder St., Colorado Springs, CO 80909
Provides information on all aspects of field hockey and USFHA activities. Because field hockey in the United States has traditionally been a woman's sport, the *Eagle* has focused on women's activities.

Female Bodybuilding. Starlog Group, Inc., 475 Park Ave., New York, NY 10016.
Focuses on body building and weight training for women.

Fighting Woman News, 1975. Box 1459, Grand Central Station, New York, NY 10163.
Features information on self-defense, martial arts, and combative sports.

Fitness Magazine, 1989. New York Times Magazine Group, 110 Fifth Ave., New York, NY 10011.
Designed to appeal to young, affluent women interested in health and fitness. Features articles on nutrition, health foods, exercise, and beauty.

Flex, 1983. 21100 Erwin St., Woodland Hills, CA 91367.
Devoted to the sport of bodybuilding; features individual profiles, nutrition, training, and ideas for workouts.

GFW (Golf for Women), 1988. Brumitt Publishers, Inc., 426 South Lamar Blvd., Oxford, MS 38655.
Provides information on selecting equipment, vacation ideas, tournament listings and results, and golf instruction.

GLOW (Gorgeous Ladies of Wrestling). Tempo Publishing Co., 475 Park Avenue, So., New York, NY 10017 (discontinued).
Featured information on professional women wrestlers.

Golf. Times-Mirror Magazines, Inc., 380 Madison Ave., New York, NY 10017.
Features instruction, individual player information, and golf articles of general interest.

Golfers' Travel Guide, 1986. RSG Publishers Inc., Box 612, Plymouth, MI 48170.
Describes golf courses in the Great Lakes states of Michigan, Ohio, Indiana, Illinois, and Wisconsin. Includes information on number of holes, par, length, and fees for both public and private courses.

Golf Traveler, 1976. Golf Card International, Inc., 1137 East 2100 So., Salt Lake City, UT 84106
Lists courses and accommodations around the nation that honor Golf Card memberships; provides some free access to courses and housing discounts for members.

Golf World, 1946. DeeBee Publishing Co., 2100 Powers Ferry Rd., Atlanta, GA 30339.
Features teaching techniques, profiles of individual players, and descriptions of golf courses. Summarizes results of competitive events.

Headway, 1985. Women's Sports Foundation, 342 Madison Ave., Suite 728, New York, NY 10173.
Provides information on all aspects of women's sports; emphasizes issues that affect women's participation and leadership opportunities in sports.

Health: The Magazine for Total Well-Being, 1969. Family Media, Inc., Women's & Fashion Group, 3 Park Ave., New York, NY 10016.
Offers information for the active, health-conscious woman. Includes health, nutrition, beauty, and related fields.

Hooks and Lines. International Women's Fishing Association, Drawer 3125, Palm Beach, FL 33480.
Includes a variety of information rleated to fishing and the IWFA

Horse Women, 1978. Rich Publishers, Inc., 41919 Moreno, 941 Calle Negocio, San Clemente, CA 92672-6202.
Features articles on English and Western riding, both amateur and professional. Covers training, nutrition, health, fashion, and careers with horses.

International Gymnast Magazine, 1956. Sundby Publications, 225 Brooks, Box G, Oceanside, CA 92054 (incorporated *Gymnastics World* and *Mademoiselle Gymnast*).

Includes instructional techniques, accomplishments of world-class gymnasts, and features on potential champions. Covers major gymnastic competitions around the world.

International Swimming Hall of Fame Headlines, 1965. One Hall of Fame Drive, Ft. Lauderdale, FL 33316.
Covers aquatics topics of all kinds and news and events of the Hall of Fame.

Journal of Physical Education, Recreation, and Dance, 1896. American Alliance for Physical Education, Recreation, and Dance, 1900 Association Drive, Reston, VA 22091 (originally *American Physical Education Review*; published under various other titles after 1930).
Includes diverse topics ranging from teaching techniques to historical and philosophical articles. Includes information on leisure activities; features articles on all subjects identified in the title.

Medicine and Science in Sports and Exercise, 1969. American College of Sports Medicine, P.O. Box 1440, Indianapolis, IN 46206.
Features a variety of research reports concerning sports medicine, especially care, treatment, and prevention of sports injuries.

Melpomene Report, 1981. Melpomene Institute for Women's Health Research, 2125 E. Hennepin Ave., Minneapolis, MN 55413.
Provides research articles, general information, profiles about physically active women; discusses relationships between lifestyle and physical activity.

Muscle and Fitness. 21100 Erwin St., Woodland Hills, CA 91367.
Emphasizes competitive bodybuilding for women and men.

Off the Glass. P.O. Box 1087, King of Prussia, PA 19406-0482.
Covers college and professional basketball.

The Olympian, 1974. 1750 E. Boulder St., Colorado Springs, CO 80909.
Features all Olympic sports; covers a variety of topics including historical essays and individual profiles.

Parachutist Magazine, 1957. 1440 Duke St., Alexandria, VA 22314.
Includes a variety of information on the sport of sky diving.

Powder, The Skier's Magazine, 1977. 33046 Calle Aviador, San Juan Capistrano, CA 92675.
Covers ski topics of all kinds including Olympic skiing, ski tours, and cross country skiing.

Runner's World, 1966. Rodale Press, Inc., 33 E. Minor St., Emmaus, PA 18409.

Focuses on running activities of all kinds; features general information about techniques, individual runners, and competition.

Running and Fitness, 1983. 9310 Old Georgetown Rd., Bethesda, MD 21814. Features information on nutrition and health, running, and other forms of aerobic exercise.

Running Times, 1977. Larry Flynt Publishers, Inc., 9171 Wilshire Blvd., Suite 300, Beverly Hills, CA 90210. Includes information about all aspects of running with a primary focus on distance running.

Scholastic Coach, 1931. Scholastic, Inc., 730 Broadway, New York, NY 10003. Focuses on diverse facets of coaching for all sports with an emphasis on team sports. A monthly feature is Women's Scene, focusing on girls' and women's sports.

Shape Magazine, 1981. 21100 Erwin St., Woodland Hills, CA 91367. Covers total fitness information for the active woman.

Side-Saddle News, 1974. International Side-Saddle Organization, Box 4076, Mt. Holly, NJ 08060. Includes a variety of topics concerning riding side-saddle, and suprisingly, perhaps, not all of the information is about women.

Skating, 1923. United States Figure Skating Association, 20 First St., Colorado Springs, CO 80906. Serves as the official publication of the United States Figure Skating Association. Profiles individual skaters, reports results of skating competitions, and provides a calendar of events concerned with skating.

Ski, 1932. Times-Mirror Magazines Inc., 2 Park Ave., New York, NY 10016. Profiles top skiers, both women and men. Features a ski clinic department for instruction; reports on ski competitions.

Skiing, 1948. P.O. Box 54180, Boulder, CO 80322-4180 Features a variety of skiing articles including competitive events, individual profiles, and instructional materials for beginning, intermediate, and advanced skiers.

Softball World, 1977. P.O. Box 10151, Grand Lake Station, Oakland, CA 94610. Covers both slow and fast pitch softball, including women's and coed play, regionally and nationally.

Sports and the Courts: Physical Education and Sports Law Quarterly. Box 2836, Winston-Salem, NC 27102.

Focuses on equity in sport, especially as it relates to women; reports on lawsuits concerning sport issues.

Sports Illustrated, 1954. Time, Inc., Time & Life Building, New York, NY 10020-1393.
Features all sports, often seasonal; articles on women are more prevalent in last two decades.

Sports 'N Spokes, 1975. 5201 N. 19th Ave., Suite 111, Phoenix, AZ 85015.
Covers wheelchair sports for women and men, both competitive and recreational.

The Sportswoman, 1925-33. Bryn Mawr, PA
Originated as the official organ of the United States Field Hockey Association; carried articles about other sports activities from its inception. Was the only regularly published periodical devoted exclusively to women's sports; contains a wealth of historical information about women's activities during the years of publication.

The Sportswoman, 1977. Charter Publishing Co., 230 Park Ave., New York, NY 10017 (discontinued).
Carried articles on a variety of sports for women, including instructional tips and reports of unusual activities in which women participate. Provided regular information about women's collegiate events.

Squash News, 1978. Squash News, Inc., Arcadia Rd., Box 52, Hope Valley, RI 02832.
Provides full coverage of amateur and professional squash, including instruction, personalities and forthcoming events.

Surfer, 1960. Surfer Publishers, 33046 Calle Aviador, San Juan Capistrano, CA 92675.
Features on surfing locales, competition, and profiles of individual surfers. Reports winners of competitive events.

Swimming World, 1960. Sports Publishers, Inc., Box 45497, Los Angeles, CA 90045.
Includes information on all aspects of competitive swimming, diving, synchronized swimming, water polo. Profiles individual swimmers; provides instructional information.

Tennis, 1929. Golf Digest/Tennis, 5520 Park Ave., P.O. Box 0395, Trumbull, CT 06611-0395.
Includes instruction, profiles of individuals, calendar of tennis events, and feature articles on a variety of tennis topics.

Tennis USA, 1979. United States Tennis Association, Family Media Inc., 3 Park Ave., New York, NY 10016 (supersedes United States Lawn Tennis Association Official News, 1928-1979).

Features a variety of tennis topics including profiles of individual players, instructional techniques, and competitive activities.

Track and Field News, 1948. 167 S. San Antonio Rd., Suite 9, Los Altos, CA 94023.

Reports information on athletic activities from high school to the Olympic Games. Includes world record data; profiles individual competitors.

Travel Fit, 1987. Box 6718, FDR Station, New York, NY 10151.

Covers fitness, jogging, squash, tennis, swimming and aerobics opportunities in fifty-seven cities nationwide.

Triathlete, 1984. 1415 Third St., Suite 303, Santa Monica, CA 90401.

Features general information related to triathlon events and endurance athletes. Includes advice about training and technique and a calendar of events.

Ultrarunning, 1981. 300 N. Main St., P.O. Box 481, Sunderland, MA 01375.

Focuses on long distance running, fifty miles and over. Features profiles of individual runners; includes race results.

United States Swimming News, 1976. U.S. Swimming, Inc., 1750 East Boulder St., Colorado Springs, CO 80909.

Highlights competitive swimming activities of all kinds with a special interest in Olympic events.

USA Gymnastics, 1960. United States Gymnastics Federation, 201 So. Capitol Ave., Suite 300, Pan American Plaza, Indianapolis, IN 46225.

Includes information about the USGF, gymnastics competition, and profiles of prominent competitors.

U.S. Archery. 1750 E. Boulder St., Colorado Springs, CO 80909.

Official publication of the National Archery Association of the United States; covers competitive events and general target archery information.

USTA College Tennis Guide, 1976. Center for Education and Recreational Tennis, 707 Alexander Rd., Princeton, NJ 08540.

Lists colleges and junior colleges offering tennis scholarships.

Volleyball Magazine, 1976. Presidio Plaza, Santa Barbara, CA 93101.

Features national and international volleyball news, teaching and coaching techniques, and information on individual players and teams.

Volleyball Monthly, 1982. Straight Down, Inc., 2308 Broad St., P.O. Box 3137, San Luis Obispo, CA 94301.
Reports on a variety of topics related to volleyball.

The Walking Magazine, 1986. 711 Boylston St., Boston, MA 02116.
Features general information on walking, either for fitness or recreation.

Water Skier, 1951. American Water Ski Association, Box 191, Winter Haven, FL 33882.
Promotes water skiing safety; features a variety of water skiing topics; serves as the official publication of the American Water Ski Association.

Woman Bowler, 1916. 5301 S. 76th St., Greendale, WI 53129.
Serves as the official publication of the Women's International Bowling Congress. Features information of all kinds from the woman's point of view. Profiles women bowlers; offers instructional tips and tournament coverage.

Women and Guns, 1989. Little River Press, 201 Paradise Point, Hot Springs, AR 71913.
Features information on pleasure shooting, different types of guns, and use of guns for self-defense; includes legislative issues and competitive events.

Women and Health: The Journal of Women's Health Care, 1978. Haworth Press, Inc., 12 West 32nd St., New York, NY 10001.
Focuses on general information of all types related to women's health issues.

Women's Coaching Clinic, 1977. 117 Cuttermill Road, Great Neck, NY 11021.
Covers coaching techniques for developing winning teams in all women's sports. Materials range from techniques of skill and strategy to the psychological aspects of coaching.

Women's Health and Fitness News, 1986. Weight Watchers Magazine, 360 Lexington Ave., New York, NY 10017.
Features general fitness and weight control information.

Women's Physique World Magazine. 19127 Wiersma St., Suite 1, Cerritos, CA 90701.
Focuses exclusively on women's bodybuilding; covers all aspects of the sport for the woman who is serious about weight training.

WomenSports, 1974. Charter Publishing Co., 230 Park Ave., New York, NY 10017 (discontinued in 1978).
Devoted to information about women and sport; published by Billie Jean King. Includes a calendar of women's sports events, early sports

heroines, winners of major sports events, and new faces in the sports scene.

Women's Sports and Fitness, 1979. Women's Sports and Fitness, Inc., 1919 14th St., Suite 421, Boulder, CO 80302 (supersedes *Women's Sports*).
Features departments that focus largely on women's fitness; includes a variety of sports articles; often profiles prominent women athletes.

Women's Track and Field World, 1982. P.O. Box 850, Cedar Glen, CA 92321.
Focuses on women's track and field news, including profiles of competitors, instructional techniques, and coaching information.

World Tennis, 1953. Family Media, Inc., 3 Park Ave., New York, NY 10016.
Includes articles on equipment, conditioning, and skill development; reports on competitive events. Offers information on instruction.

Sports Organizations

AEROBICS AND FITNESS ASSOCIATION OF AMERICA, 1983. 15250 Ventura Blvd., Suite 310, Sherman Oaks, CA 91403.
Conducts workshops and seminars for aerobics instructors; offers insurance and job referral service; determines standards for aerobics competition.

AFFILIATED NATIONAL RIDING COMMISSION, 1900 Association Dr., Reston, VA 22091.
Sponsors seminars, clinics, and competition to encourage the sport of horseback riding.

ALLIANCE OF WOMEN BIKERS, 1977. P.O. Box 484, Eau Claire, WI 54702.
Encourages motorcycling for women; attempts to dispel ideas that motorcycling is only a tough, macho activity.

AMATEUR ATHLETIC UNION, 1888. P.O. Box 68207, 3400 West 86th St., Indianapolis, IN 46268.
Sponsors Junior Olympics, Chrysler Fund/AAU Physical Fitness Program, and senior sports programs.

AMATEUR SKATING UNION OF THE UNITED STATES, 1928. 1033 Shady Lane, Glen Ellyn, IL 60137.
Promotes amateur ice skating, speed and racing, in the United States.

AMATEUR SOFTBALL ASSOCIATION, 1933. 2801 Northeast 50th St., Oklahoma City, OK 73111.

Serves as the governing body for softball in the United States. Promotes the sport for girls, boys, women, and men.

AMATEUR TRAPSHOOTING ASSOCIATION, 1923. 601 W. National Rd., Vandalia, OH 45377.

Determines rules for trapshooting competition; maintains records for registered class competitions.

AMERICAN ATHLETIC ASSOCIATION FOR THE DEAF, 1945. 1134 Davenport Dr., Burton, MI 48529.

Promotes athletic competition and recreational sports for the deaf. Sponsors the World Games for the deaf.

AMERICAN BLIND BOWLING ASSOCIATION, 1951. 67 Bame Ave., Buffalo, NY 14215.

Promotes recreational bowling for legally blind adults.

AMERICAN CANOE ASSOCIATION, 1880. P.O. Box 1190, Newington, VA 22122.

Serves as the governing body for canoeing and kayaking in the United States. Promotes safety; sponsors educational programs.

AMERICAN COLLEGE OF SPORTS MEDICINE, 1954. P.O. Box 1440, 401 W. Michigan St., Indianapolis, IN 46206-1440.

Promotes research in sports, exercise, and general health; reports information concerning adaptations and responses to exercise. Includes other health aspects related to participation in sport and exercise.

AMERICAN PLATFORM TENNIS ASSOCIATION, 1931. Box 901, Upper Montclair, NJ 07043.

Promotes the game of platform tennis; sanctions tournaments; provides officials for competition.

AMERICAN RUNNING AND FITNESS ASSOCIATION, 1968. 9310 Old Georgetown Rd., Bethesda, MD 20814 (supersedes National Jogging Association).

Encourages running and other aerobic fitness activities; provides information about fitness and running; reports research on exercise physiology.

AMERICAN SKI ASSOCIATION, 1976. 1888 Sherman, Suite 500, Denver, CO 80203.

Provides information about ski conditions; arranges accommodations at ski areas; provides financial assistance for teaching skiing to the disabled.

AMERICAN TURNERS, 1848. 2503 S. Preston St., P.O. Box 1735, Louisville, KY 40217.

Promotes family health and physical activity; sponsors national competition in gymnastics, basketball, volleyball, softball, swimming, and bowling.

AMERICAN WATER SKI ASSOCIATION, 1939. P.O. Box 191, Winter Haven, FL 33882.
Promotes recreational and competitive water skiing in the United States; establishes rules for competition.

AMERICAN YOUTH HOSTELS, 1934. P.O. Box 37613, Washington, DC 20013.
Sponsors inexpensive recreation and travel opportunities; maintains low-cost accommodations throughout the United States. Sponsors hiking, cycling, canoeing, and skiing trips in the United States and abroad.

APPALACHIAN MOUNTAIN CLUB, 1876. Five Joy St., Boston, MA 02108.
Promotes enjoyment of the outdoors; conducts educational programs; maintains a large mountaineering library.

ASSOCIATION FOR FITNESS IN BUSINESS, 1974. 310 N. Alabama, Indianapolis, IN 46204.
Promotes development of fitness programs in business and industry. Sponsors educational programs and stimulates research in fitness area.

THE ATHLETICS CONGRESS OF THE USA, 1979. 200 S. Capitol Ave., Suite 140, Indianapolis, IN 46225.
Promotes amateur athletics in the United States. Sanctions competitions; serves as the governing body for track and field, long-distance running, and racewalking. Conducts training and development programs. Maintains women's committees for track and field, racewalking, and long-distance running.

BASS'N GAL, 1976. P.O. Box 13925, 2007 Roosevelt, Arlington, TX 76013.
Promotes public awareness of bass fishing as a major sport as well as a recreational activity for women; strives to dispel myths about women's ability to compete on a par with men.

BLACK TENNIS AND SPORTS FOUNDATION, 1977. 1893 Amsterdam Ave., New York, NY 10032.
Provides support and resources for black and minority youth; organizes tennis teams; sponsors annual Arthur Ashe/Althea Gibson Tennis Classic.

BOYS AND GIRLS INTERNATIONAL FLOOR HOCKEY, 1963. P.O. Box 1653, Battle Creek, MI 49016.

Promotes recreational and educational floor hockey programs for girls and boys in grades three through six; sponsors a championship tournament.

CAMPING WOMEN, 1976. 625 W. Cornell Ave., Fresno, CA 93705.
Promotes outdoor activities for developing camping abilities and a comfortable feeling for women in the out-of-doors.

CINDERELLA SOFTBALL LEAGUE, 1958. P.O. Box 1411, Corning, NY 14830.
Promotes softball for girls, age eighteen and younger; regulates and sponsors the annual Cinderella World Series.

EASTERN WOMEN'S AMATEUR BASKETBALL LEAGUE OF THE AAU, 1970. 14206 Day Farm Rd., Glenelg, MD 21737.
Encourages basketball involvement for high school and college athletes after finishing school play; sponsors tournament competition.

FEMINIST KARATE UNION, 1971. 5429 Russell Ave., N.W., Seattle, WA 98107.
Promotes development of karate and self-defense skills for women.

FIFTY-PLUS RUNNERS ASSOCIATION, 1980. P.O. Box D, Stanford, CA 94309.
Promotes exchange of information about the benefits of running for women and men over fifty years of age. Organizes occasional regional runs.

GEORGE KHOURY ASSOCIATION OF BASEBALL LEAGUES, 1936. 5400 Meramec Bottom Rd., St. Louis, MO 63128.
Sponsors baseball and softball for girls and boys seven years of age and up. Uses altered rules to accommodate size and ability of players; conducts play-off tournaments at the end of the season.

ICE SKATING INSTITUTE OF AMERICA, 1959. 1000 Skokie Blvd., Wilmette, IL 60091-1198.
Promotes interest in recreational ice skating; includes both amateur and professional skaters.

INTERCOLLEGIATE SOCCER ASSOCIATION OF AMERICA, 1924. 417 S. 14th St., Quincy, IL 62301.
Promotes college soccer for both women and men; sponsors research at colleges and universities.

INTERNATIONAL ACADEMY OF AQUATIC ART, 1955. 2360 Hedge Row, Northfield, IL 60093.

Encourages interest and participation in aquatic art, an outgrowth of synchronized swimming, water ballet, and other aquatic activities; conducts educational programs on aquatic art techniques.

INTERNATIONAL DANCE-EXERCISE ASSOCIATION, 1982. 4120 Cornerstone Court, San Diego, CA 92121.
Promotes safety in exercise of all kinds; concerned with needs of individuals in slimnastics, jazz exercise, and aerobics.

INTERNATIONAL SIDE-SADDLE ORGANIZATION, 1974. P.O. Box 4076, Mt. Holly, NJ 08060
Sponsors women's side-saddle horse shows; conducts educational clinics for training in side-saddle riding.

INTERNATIONAL WOMEN'S BOARDSAILING ASSOCIATION, 1982. P.O. Box 44549, Washington, DC 20026.
Supports both amateur and professional boardsailing for women. Promotes status of competitive boardsailing through improved conditions for competition and higher prize monies.

INTERNATIONAL WOMEN'S FISHING ASSOCIATION, 1955. P.O. Drawer 3125, Palm Beach, FL 33480.
Promotes angling competition of all kinds for women.

LADIES KENNEL ASSOCIATION OF AMERICA, 1901. 320 Sunrise Dr., Arroyo Grande, CA 93420.
Encourages sound purebred breeding practices; holds annual all-breed dog show.

LADIES PROFESSIONAL BOWLERS TOUR, 1981. 7171 Cherryvale Blvd., Rockford, IL 61112 (supersedes Professional Bowlers Association).
Sponsors championship professional bowling tournaments; maintains members' career competition statistics.

LADIES PROFESSIONAL GOLF ASSOCIATION, 1950. 4675 Sweetwater Blvd., Sugar Land, TX 77479.
Maintains member's statistics on money winnings and tournament championships; assists women in securing golf positions.

MAJOR LEAGUE VOLLEYBALL, 1986. 333 Twin Dolphin Dr., Suite 600, Redwood City, CA 94065.
Organized as a league of female professional volleyball players.

MELPOMENE INSTITUTE FOR WOMEN'S HEALTH RESEARCH, 1981. 2125 E. Hennepin Ave., Minneapolis, MN 55413.

Focuses primarily on issues related to girls' and women's sport and physical activity. Researches topics such as athletic amenorrhea, osteosporosis, and exercise and pregnancy.

MOTORMAIDS, INC., 1941. P.O. Box 443, Chardon, OH 44024.
Promotes motorcycling activities of all kinds for women.

THE MOUNTAINEERS, 1906. 300 Third Ave., W., Seattle, WA 98119.
Conducts trips for members; sponsors safety training; maintains a museum and library.

NATIONAL AMATEUR BOWLER INC., 1980. P.O. Box 17-1610, Kansas City, KS 66117.
Sponsors bowling tournaments throughout the United States for women and men whose bowling averages are 199 or less.

NATIONAL ARCHERY ASSOCIATION OF THE U.S., 1879. 1705 E. Boulder St., Colorado Springs, CO 80909.
Sponsors archery competition; standardizes rules; keeps official records of archery events.

NATIONAL ASSOCIATION FOR GIRLS AND WOMEN IN SPORT, 1899. 1900 Association Dr., Reston, VA 22091.
Supports and promotes quality sports programs for girls and women. Publishes official rule books for many women's sports.

NATIONAL ASSOCIATION OF INTERCOLLEGIATE ATHLETICS, 1940. 1221 Baltimore, Kansas City, MO 64105.
Sponsors national women's and men's championships for member schools; conducts workshops and clinics for athletic directors and coaches; devlops rules and standards for competition.

NATIONAL ATHLETIC TRAINERS' ASSOCIATION, 1950. 1001 E. Fourth St., Greenville, NC 27858.
Promotes safe participation in competitive athletics and continued improvement of the athletic training profession.

NATIONAL COLLEGIATE ATHLETIC ASSOCIATION, 1906. Nall Ave. at 63rd St., Mission, KS 66201.
Sponsors national championships for member schools; establishes rules governing all sports competition for college women and men.

NATIONAL DEAF WOMEN'S BOWLING ASSOCIATION. 33 August Rd., Simsbury, CT 06070.
Promotes bowling opportunities for women with hearing impairments.

NATIONAL FEDERATION OF STATE HIGH SCHOOL ASSOCIATIONS, 1920. P.O. Box 20626, 11724 Plaza Circle, Kansas City, MO 64195.

Coordinates activities of state high school athletic associations. Supervises interstate athletic interests of high schools; maintains a national press service.

NATIONAL FIELD ARCHERY ASSOCIATION, 1939. 31407 Outer 1-10, Redlands, CA 92373.

Promotes educational programs and national competition in field archery events for women and men.

NATIONAL FOUNDATION OF WHEELCHAIR TENNIS, 1980. 940 Calle Amanecer, Suite B, San Clemente, CA 92672.

Sponsors clinics and wheelchair tennis tournaments; promotes wheelchair tennis for the disabled.

NATIONAL HANDICAPPED SPORTS AND RECREATION ASSOCIATION, 1967. 1145 19th St., N.W., Suite 717, Washington, DC 20036.

Promotes sports and leisure opportunities for individuals with visual and mobility handicaps. Conducts national clinics for teaching adaptive sports activities.

NATIONAL INTERCOLLEGIATE WOMEN'S FENCING ASSOCIATION, 1929. 235 McCosh Rd., Upper Montclair, NJ 07043.

Promotes women's fencing in colleges and universities; sponsors workshops, clinics, and competitive fencing matches.

NATIONAL RECREATION AND PARK ASSOCIATION, 1965. 3101 Park Center Dr., Alexandria, VA 22302.

Sponsors educational programs concerned with parks and recreation; promotes leisure values; works toward improvement of parks and recreational areas.

NATIONAL RIFLE ASSOCIATION, 1871. 1600 Rhode Island Ave., N.W., Washington, DC 20036.

Promotes firearms safety; sponstor teams for world championship competition; maintains records of national and international competition.

NATIONAL SENIOR WOMEN'S TENNIS ASSOCIATION, 1974. 329 Wigmore Dr., Pasadena, CA 91105.

Sponsors tennis events for women age thirty-five and over; conducts a national team competition.

NATIONAL SKEET SHOOTING ASSOCIATION, 1935. P.O. Box 680007, San Antonio, TX 78268.

Formulates rules for and supervises competitive shoots. Recognizes achievements of outstanding shooters.

NATIONAL WHEELCHAIR ATHLETIC ASSOCIATION, 1958. 1604 E. Pikes Peak Ave., Colorado Springs, CO 80909.

Sponsors regional competition for women and men in wheelchair sports; conducts the annual National Wheelchair Games.

NATIONAL WOMEN'S HEALTH NETWORK, 1976. 1325 G St., N.W., Washington, DC 20005

Concerned with the women's health movement, including federal health policy and feminist health projects.

NATIONAL WOMEN'S MARTIAL ARTS FEDERATION, 1972. 1724 Sillview Dr., Pittsburgh, PA 15243.

Encourages women's participation in the martial arts; presents workshops and training camps to develop skills in the activities; sponsors competitive events.

NINETY-NINES, INTERNATIONAL WOMEN PILOTS, 1929. Will Rogers Airport, P.O. Box 59965, Oklahoma City, OK 73159.

Sponsors educational programs focusing on safety and a better understanding of aviation; maintains a library and resource center, including biographical archives and a placement service.

NORTH AMERICAN NETWORK OF WOMEN RUNNERS, 1979. P.O. Box 719, Bala Cynwyd, PA 19004.

Promotes low-cost running opportunities for women; interested in making good health, athletics, and physical fitness available to all women.

NOW LEGAL DEFENSE AND EDUCATIONAL FUND, 1970. 99 Hudson St., 12th Floor, New York, NY 10013.

Provides legal assistance to women, especially for gender discrimination and equal rights issues. Conducts research and publishes data pertinent to the legal, economic, and educational status of women.

PROFESSIONAL SKATERS GUILD OF AMERICA, 1938. P.O. Box 5904, Rochester, MN 55903.

Promotes figure skating in the United States; maintains high standards of professional and ethical conduct in skating.

ROAD RUNNERS CLUB OF AMERICA, 1958. 629 S. Washington St., Alexandria, VA 22314.

Promotes distance running; sponsors fun runs, races, and running for fitness. Includes a Women's Distance Festival program.

SCHOLASTIC ROWING ASSOCIATION OF AMERICA, 1933. 120 United States Ave., Gibbsboro, NJ 08026.
Promotes interest in rowing for school girls and boys. Sponsors an annual amateur regatta.

SPECIAL OLYMPICS INTERNATIONAL, 1968. 1350 New York Ave., N.W., Suite 500, Washington, DC 20005.
Promotes athletic competition, physical fitness, and sports participation for mentally retarded persons. Conducts Special Olympics competition all over the world.

UNITED STATES AMATEUR CONFEDERATION OF ROLLER SKATING, 1937. 1500 S. 705th St., P.O. Box 83067, Lincoln, NE 68506.
Serves as the national governing body for the sport of roller skating. Sponsors training camps; sanctions artistic, hockey, and speed competitions in the United States.

UNITED STATES ASSOCIATION FOR BLIND ATHLETES, 1976. 4708 46th St., N.W., Washington, DC 20016.
Focuses on sports for the visually impaired. Promotes independence through athletic participation; organizes regional and national competition in various sports.

UNITED STATES BADMINTON ASSOCIATION, 1936. 501 W. Sixth St., Papillion, NE 68046.
Acts as the national governing body for badminton in the United States; codifies rules and conducts competition.

UNITED STATES CROQUET ASSOCIATION, 1976. 500 Avenue of Champions, Palm Beach Gardens, FL 33418.
Encourages interest in croquet; sponsors district, regional, state, and national championships.

UNITED STATES CURLING ASSOCIATION, 1958. 1100 Centerpoint Dr., Stevens Point, WI 54481.
Organizes and promotes curling activities in the United States. Sanctions women's, men's, and mixed curling competitions.

UNITED STATES CYCLING FEDERATION, 1921. c/o USOC, 1750 E. Boulder St., Colorado Springs, CO 80909.
Governs amateur cycling in the United States and all bicycling competition; sponsors national competition.

UNITED STATES FENCING ASSOCIATION, 1893. 1750 E. Boulder St., Colorado Springs, CO 80909.
Promotes growth and development of fencing in the United States. Selects members of the Olympic fencing team.

UNITED STATES FIELD HOCKEY ASSOCIATION, 1921. 1750 E. Boulder St., Colorado Springs, CO 80909.
Governs women's field hockey in the United States; promotes interest in the sport; sponsors national tournaments.

UNITED STATES FIGURE SKATING ASSOCIATION, 1921. 201 1st St., Colorado Springs, CO 80906.
Governs the sport of amateur figure skating in the United States.

UNITED STATES GYMNASTICS FEDERATION, 1963. Pan American Plaza, 201 S. Capitol Ave., Suite 300, Indianapolis, IN 46225.
Governs amateur gymnastics in the United States; conducts and sanctions national competitions.

UNITED STATES HANG GLIDING ASSOCIATION, 1971. P.O. Box 8300, Colorado Springs, CO 80907.
Promotes safety education in the sport of hang gliding, conducts training clinics, and sponsors competition.

UNITED STATES JUDO ASSOCIATION, 1954. 19 N. Union Blvd., Colorado Springs, CO 80909.
Encourages participation in judo, both recreationally and competitively. Recognizes outstanding and most improved female and male judo athletes.

UNITED STATES PADDLE TENNIS ASSOCIATION, 1923. 189 Seeley St., Brooklyn, NY 11218.
Encourages the popularity of paddle tennis; standardizes rules; conducts national tournaments.

UNITED STATES PARACHUTE ASSOCIATION, 1957. 1440 Duke St., Alexandria, VA 22314.
Promotes the sport of sky diving; encourages competition, record attempts, and training in the sport.

UNITED STATES ROWING ASSOCIATION, 1872. 201 S. Capitol Ave., Indianapolis, IN 46225.
Promotes amateur rowing in the United States; sponsors annual women's, men's and master's championship regattas. Selects all rowing crews who represent the United States in the World, Olympic, and Pan American Games.

UNITED STATES SENIOR ATHLETIC GAMES, 1979. 200 Castlewood Dr., North Palm Beach, FL 33408.
Encourages athletic participaton and competition for adults. Sponsors Senior Athletic Games.

UNITED STATES SKI ASSOCIATION, 1904. 1500 Kearns Blvd., Highway 248, Bldg. E/F, Suite F200, Park City, UT 84060.
Provides training projects, coaching, and competition at regional, national, and international levels. Encompasses Nordic and Alpine recreational skiing and competition and freestyle skiing. Serves as the official governing body for skiing in the United States.

UNITED STATES SOCCER FEDERATION, 1913. 1750 E. Boulder St., Colorado Springs, CO 80909.
Governs the sport of soccer in the United States. Conducts clinics and competitions; manages National Women's Amateur Cup.

UNITED STATES SYNCHRONIZED SWIMMING, INC., 1980. Pan American Plaza, 201 S. Capitol Ave., Plaza Suite 510, Indianapolis, IN 46225.
Sponsors synchronized swimming competition; presents educational programs for officials, swimmers, and coaches. Selects United States athletes for international competition.

UNITED STATES TENNIS ASSOCIATION, 1881. 1212 Avenue of the Americas, New York, NY 10036
Sanctions innumerable tennis tournaments for all ages; sponsors national championship competition, a junior program for girls and boys, and adult recreational leagues.

UNITED STATES VOLLEYBALL ASSOCIATION, 1928. 1750 E. Boulder St., Colorado Springs, CO 80909.
Organizes and promotes the sport of volleyball at all levels. Serves as the national governing body for United States volleyball.

UNITED STATES WOMEN'S CURLING ASSOCIATION, 1947. 4114 N. 53rd St., Omaha, NE 68104.
Maintains records of association competition and awards. Is affiliated with the United States Curling Association.

UNITED STATES WOMEN'S LACROSSE ASSOCIATION, 1931. 20 E. Sunset Ave., Philadelphia, PA 19118.
Promotes women's lacrosse, sponsors an annual national tournament, and determines rules for competition.

UNITED STATES WOMEN'S TRACK COACHES ASSOCIATION, 1967. Belmont 606, University of Texas, Austin, TX 78712.
Provides information on women's track and field especially pertinent to competitive programs.

WOMEN'S ALL-STAR ASSOCIATION, 1971. 29 Garey Dr., Chappaqua, NY 10514.

Sponsors bowling tournaments for amateur women aged seventeen and older; publicizes women bowlers and their accomplishments.

WOMEN'S BASKETBALL COACHES ASSOCIATION, 1981. 1687 Tullie Circle, Suite 127, Atlanta, GA 30329.
Promotes amateur basketball competition at national and international levels; sponsors educational programs and national clinics.

WOMEN'S EQUITY ACTION LEAGUE, 1968. 1250 I St., N.W., Suite 305, Washington, DC 20005.
Sponsors programs of research, education and legislative advocacy to ensure economic and legal rights for women.

WOMEN IN SOCCER, 1979. 242 E. 75th St., New York, NY 10021.
Promotes soccer for girls and women in the New York area.

WOMEN ON WHEELS, 1982. P.O. Box 14187, Phoenix, AZ 85063.
Promotes recognition of women motorcyclists, especially in the motorcycle industry; sponsors safety education programs.

WOMEN'S INTERNATIONAL BOWLING CONGRESS, 1916. 5301 S. 76th St., Greendale, WI 53129.
Sanctions bowling for women throughout the United States, Canada, Puerto Rico, Bermuda, and several other foreign countries. Sponsors an annual championship tournament and maintains statistical information pertaining to competition.

WOMEN'S INTERNATIONAL MOTORCYCLE ASSOCIATION, 1950. 360 E. Main St., Waterloo, NY 13165.
Promotes women's motorcycle racing.

WOMEN'S INTERNATIONAL SURFING ASSOCIATION, 1975. 30202 Silver Spur Rd., P.O. Box 512, San Juan Capistrano, CA 92693.
Promotes the sport of surfing for women; sponsors instructional programs and surfing competitions.

WOMEN'S INTERNATIONAL TENNIS ASSOCIATION, 1973. Grand Bay Plaza, 2665 S. Bayshore Dr., Suite 1002, Miami, FL 33133.
Organizes professional women's tennis tournaments.

WOMEN OUTDOORS, 1980. Curtis Hall, 474 Boston Ave., Medford, MA 02155.
Maintains a network of women with outdoor interests; holds training programs for women to develop outdoor skills.

WOMEN'S PROFESSIONAL RACQUETBALL ASSOCIATION, 1979. 1001 C.N. Harlem, Oak Park, IL 60302.

Sponsors a professional racquetball tournament for women; supervises all sanctioned tournaments.

WOMEN'S PROFESSIONAL RODEO ASSOCIATION, 1948. Rt. 5, Box 698, Blanchard, OK 73010 (supersedes Girls' Rodeo Association).
Sponsors clinics on fundamental horsemanship skills and rodeo events. Awards monetary prizes to the top barrel racers and to the champions of the six sanctioned rodeo events for women.

WOMEN'S PROFESSIONAL SKI RACING, INC., 1977. 75 Ash St., Weston, MA 02193.
Sponsors the Women's Professional Ski Racing Tour; sanctions pro ski races for women.

WOMEN'S SPORTS FOUNDATION, 1974. 342 Madison Ave., Suite 728, New York, NY 10017.
Promotes women's participation in all sports activities; conducts educational seminars; presents awards for outstanding achievements in women's sports.

WOODSWOMEN, 1977. 25 W. Diamond Lake Rd., Minneapolis, MN 55419.
Promotes a variety of outdoor activities for women, including mountaineering, backpacking, canoeing. Sponsors educational programs; conducts wilderness trips.

WORLDWIDE WOMEN PROFESSIONAL BOWLERS, 1965. 8523 Lindley Ave., Northridge, CA 91325.
Encourages women to become involved in bowling and competition; sponsors bowling tournaments.

YOUNG AMERICAN BOWLING ALLIANCE, 1982. 5301 S. 76th St., Greendale, WI 53129.
Promotes tournament competition and encourages bowling for girls and boys aged twenty one and under. Includes a Pee Wee membership for bowlers aged three to seven.

Halls of Fame

AMATEUR SPORTS HALL OF FAME. 301 Central Ave., Johnstown, PA 15902.
Recognizes outstanding amateur athletes in all sports.

AMATEUR TRAPSHOOTING ASSOCIATION HALL OF FAME, 1969. 601 W. National, Vandalia, OH 45377.

Honors persons who have contributed to the growth of trapshooting and to the betterment of the sport, and shooters who have made impressive records in trapshooting.

AMERICAN BICYCLE HALL OF FAME, 1968. 260 W. 260th St., New York, NY 10471.

Honors individuals who have contributed to or excelled in bicycling.

ARCHERY HALL OF FAME, 1972. Fred Bear Museum, Bear Mountain, Grayling, MI 49738.

Includes honorees who have excelled in shooting or have made significant contributions to the sport of archery.

CITIZENS SAVINGS ATHLETIC FOUNDATION (formerly HELMS ATHLETIC FOUNDATION), 1936. 9800 S. Sepulveda Blvd., Los Angeles, CA 90045.

Houses thirty-one separate sports halls of fame. Recognizes outstanding invididuals in each specific area. Maintains a library for all sports.

HALL OF FAME OF THE AMATEUR SKATING UNION OF THE UNITED STATES, 1972. 375 Washington St., Newburgh, NY 12550.

Honors speed skaters who have completed their competitive career. Eligible skaters are those who have won a medal in the Olympic Games or World meets, have set two records, or won two national championships.

ICE SKATING HALL OF FAME, 1963. 1000 Skokie Blvd., Wilmette, IL 60091.

Honors persons who have made national contributions to the sport of ice skating in the form of participation, teaching, judging, facility development, or promotion of skating through published books.

INTERNATIONAL WOMEN'S SPORTS HALL OF FAME, 1980. 342 Madison Ave., Suite 728, New York, NY 10173.

Recognizes women who have achieved outstanding athletic success, have longevity in sport, or who have made significant contributions to the development of women's sport. Includes two groups, the pioneers who are pre-1960, and the contemporaries.

INTERNATIONAL SWIMMING HALL OF FAME, 1968. 1 Hall of Fame Drive, Fort Lauderdale, FL 33316.

Recognizes swimmers, divers, and coaches who have achieved success in their areas and other individuals who have made significant contributions to the sport. Maintains a library of books, films, rare books and a special reference section for research.

INTERNATIONAL TENNIS HALL OF FAME, 1954. 194 Bellevue Ave., Newport, RI 02840.

Honors outstanding champions in the sport and persons who have made significant contributions in other ways to the sport of tennis. The Tennis Museum, affiliated with the hall of fame, has a special display of one hundred years of women's tennis fashions.

LADIES PROFESSIONAL GOLF HALL OF FAME, 1967. Augusta Golf and Country Club, Augusta, GA 30903.

Recognizes persons who have achieved success in professional golf or who have contributed to the development of the sport.

NAISMITH MEMORIAL BASKETBALL HALL OF FAME, 1959. 1150 W. Columbus Ave., P.O. Box 179, Springfield, MA 01109.

Recognizes individuals and teams who have excelled in the sport of basketball or who have made significant contributions to the sport. Includes honorees from high school, college, amateur, professional and military teams.

NATIONAL ASSOCIATION OF LEFT-HANDED GOLFERS HALL OF FAME, 1961. P.O. Box 489, Camden, SC 29020.

Honors left-handed golfers with consistent playing records.

NATIONAL BASEBALL HALL OF FAME AND MUSEUM, 1939. Cooperstown, NY 13326.

Offers a display honoring women umpires, women owners of baseball teams, and women members of the All American Girls' Professional Baseball League, in operation from 1943 to 1954.

NATIONAL COWBOY HALL OF FAME AND HERITAGE CENTER. 1700 N.E. 63rd St., Oklahoma City, OK 49849.

Inducts individuals who have achieved success in rodeo; includes women who were very early rodeo participants.

NATIONAL COWGIRL HALL OF FAME AND WESTERN HERITAGE CENTER, 1975. P.O. Box 1742, Hereford, TX 79045.

Honors women who have achieved success as trick riders, trick ropers, rodeo participants, or as ranchwomen. Includes women who have made significant contributions in establishing the West.

NATIONAL HIGH SCHOOL SPORTS HALL OF FAME, 1982. 11724 Plaza Circle, Box 20626, Kansas City, MO 64195.

Honors individuals who have achieved excellence in sports as a coach, athlete, administrator, or official.

NATIONAL SHUFFLEBOARD HALL OF FAME, 1970. Shuffleboard Club, Mirror Lake Drive, St. Petersburg, FL 33701.

Recognizes individuals who promote the game of shuffleboard or who excel in competition.

NATIONAL SKI HALL OF FAME, 1954. P.O. Box 191, Ishpeming, MI 49849.

Automatically inducts medal winners in the Olympic Games; honors athletes and other individuals who have made significant contributions to the sport.

NATIONAL SOFTBALL HALL OF FAME, 1957. 2801 Northeast 50th St., Oklahoma City, OK 73111.

Recognizes women and men who have distinguished themselves in amateur softball or have contributed to the growth and development of the sport. Both slow-pitch and fast-pitch players are eligible.

NATIONAL TRACK AND FIELD HALL OF FAME, 1974. One Hoosier Dome, Indianapolis, IN 46225.

Honors athletes who have achieved excellence in track and field competition; inducts outstanding coaches and individuals who have made significant contributions to the sport.

ROLLER SKATING HALL OF FAME, 1983. 7700 A St., P.O. Box 81846, Lincoln, NE 68501.

Affiliated with the United States Amateur Confederation of Roller Skating; honors persons recognized as outstanding performers or contributors to the the sport of roller skating.

TRAPSHOOTING HALL OF FAME AND MUSEUM, 1969. 601 W. National, Vandalia, OH 45377.

Honors persons who have made outstanding records in shooting or have contributed to the development of the sport.

UNITED STATES FIGURE SKATING HALL OF FAME, 1975. Sears Crescent, Suite 500, City Hall Plaza, Boston, MA 02108.

Includes amateur and professional skaters who have achieved success and persons who have made significant contributions to figure skating.

UNITED STATES ROWING HALL OF FAME, 1976. 201 S. Capitol Ave., Indianapolis, IN 46225.

Honors individuals who have been elite competitors in the sport of rowing.

UNITED STATES TRACK AND FIELD HALL OF FAME, 1972. P.O. Box 297, Angola, IN 46703.

Honors women and men who have brought distinction to themselves as well as to the sport of track and field.

WATER SKI MUSEUM AND HALL OF FAME, 1982. 799 Overlook Dr., Winter Haven, FL 33884-1671.

> Inducts individuals who have contributed to the sport of water skiing as a participant, competitor, or ways other than as an athlete.

WHEELCHAIR SPORTS HALL OF FAME, 1970. 40-24 62d St., Woodside, NY 11377.

> Honors wheelchair athletes who have had outstanding performances in national and international competition; recognizes persons who have achieved success through coaching or administration.

WOMEN'S GOLF HALL OF FAME, 1974. P.O. Box 908, Pinehurst, NC 28374.

> Recognizes both amateur and professional players and other persons who have supported the development of golf. Selects members from the three categories of players up to 1930, modern players, and promoters of golf.

WOMEN'S INTERNATIONAL BOWLING CONGRESS HALL OF FAME, 5301 S. 76th St., Greendale, WI 53129.

> Elects members in three categories: past bowling achievement, service, and current significant individual bowling achievement.

WOMEN'S PROFESSIONAL BILLIARD ALLIANCE HALL OF FAME, 1975. 17 Strong Pl., Brooklyn, NY 11231.

> Honors females in the sport of billiards, both players and contributors to the sport.

Author Index

Subject Index

Acrobatics, 1936.1
Addie, Pauline Betz, 1949.2, 1953.2,
    1985.8
Aerobic(s), 1972.3
    exercises, 1983.18, 1986.3
Aikido, 1972.11
Albright, Tenley, 1928.5, 1976.5,
    1978.6, 1981.2, 1981.25
    and Olympics, 1980.13
All-American Girls Baseball League,
    1978.11
Amateurism, 1964.5
Amateur spirit in tennis, 1975.6
American Alliance for Health,
    Physical Education, and
    Recreation, 1977.1, 1977.13,
    1978.33
American Physical Education
    Association, 1978.33
American sportswomen, 1983.15
American Women's Himalayan
    Expedition, 1980.1
Andersen, Greta, 1977.6
Androgyny, 1981.7
Annapurna Mountains, 1980.1
    and American Women, 1980.24
Anthony, Julie, 1976.12
Applebee, Constance, 1961.1

Archery, 1936.1, 1955.4
    and female body frame, 1982.11
    manual, 1971.1
    techniques, 1943.1, 1947.1, 1960.4
Ashford, Evelyn, 1981.30
Association of Intercollegiate
    Athletics for Women (AIAW),
    1986.8
Aussem, Cilli, 1949.2, 1971.2
Austin, Tracy, 1978.36, 1979.15,
    1981.1
    tennis player, 1978.41
Automobile land speed records,
    1980.23
Automobile racing, 1958.4
    and Janet Guthrie, 1978.17,
    1978.40, 1981.10
    women and, 1965.7
Aviation, 1928.3, 1987.9, 1989.7

Babashoff, Shirley, 1975.9
    swimmer, 1975.13
Babilonia, Tai, 1978.26
Backpacking, 1982.11
Bacon, Mary, 1973.6
Badminton, 28, 1943.1, 1955.4,
    1974.12, 1985.15
    manual, 1971.1

189

Men's varsity crew, 1981.5
Merki, Nancy, 1952.1
Meyer, Debbie, 1972.9
Mills, Mary, 1973.4
Mittermaier, Rosi, 1977.36
Moody, Helen Wills, 1964.6, 1965.3,
    1971.7, 1972.6, 1973.11, 1975.35,
    1976.5, 1979.12, 1979.27, 1981.1,
    1981.2, 1981.25, 1987.6, 1989.11
    Forest Hills champion, 1976.23
    and Olympics, 1980.13
    Wightman Cup winner, 1978.13
Moran, Gertrude "Gussie," 1928.5,
    1961.6, 1985.8
    singles champion, 1975.28
Morin, Nea, 1968.6
Morrissey, Muriel, 1987.9
Mortimer, Angela, 1962.1
Motorcycle, 1976.3
Mountain climbing, 1958.1, 1968.6,
    1990.2
    and Hulda Crooks, 1980.11
    myths, 1979.35
Mt. Everest expedition, 1973.20
Muldowney, Barbara, 1975.40
Muldowney, Shirley, 1977.19
Mulhall, Lucille, 1955.1

Nagel, Judy, 1977.45
National Association for Girls and
    Women's Sports, 1975.1
National Singles, 1978.13
National Women's Football League,
    1985.3
Nautilus exercise machines, 1983.7,
    1983.18
Navratilova, Martina, 1976.12,
    1979.12, 1981.1, 1987.6, 1988.20,
    1988.22
Neal, Patsy, 1969.10
Nelson, Cindy, 1975.13, 1977.16
Nelson, Marjorie, 1986.7
Nesvkaitis, Violetta, 1975.38
Nichols, Ruth, 1932.1
Nuthall, Betty, 1949.2
Nyad, Diana, 1975.9

Oakley, Annie, 1954.2, 1979.2
Oberlin College, 1976.16

O'Donnell, Gladys, 1942.1
Olympiad, 1984.8, 1988.7
Olympics,
    Ancient, 1979.29, 1979.36, 1984.8
    and gymnastics, 1976.9
    medal winners, 1984.17
    and track and field, 1988.7
Olympic Training Center, 1986.20,
    1988.17
Omlie, Phoebe, 1936.1
O'Neil, Kitty, 1980.23
    wonder woman, 1981.17
Oxbridge Women's College, 1988.11

Paddle tennis, 1933.1, 1958.3
Palfrey, Sarah, 1985.8
Palmer, Sandy, 1973.4
Parachute jumping, 1979.24
Parry, Zale, 1976.13
Patterson, Shirley, 1977.19
Peck, Annie, 1981.17
Pentathlon, 1970.11, 1977.14
Peppler, Mary Jo, 1977.19
Peters, Mary, 1980.28
Petticoat pioneers, 1973.20
Physical defense, 1976.36
Physical education, 1937.1
    and the handicapped, 1974.26
    program, 1927.2, 1934.1, 1938.1,
    1973.9
    and women, 1928.4, 1930.1,
    1961.1, 1979.34, 1983.12,
    1983.14
Polo player, 1978.22
Proell, Annemarie Moser, 1975.14
Putnam, George, 1989.7

Quimby, Harriet, 1942.1

Race Across America Competition,
    1988.10
Racing flyer, 1942.1
Racquetball, 1974.12, 1980.29
Rankin, Judy, 1973.4, 1977.16
Rawls, Katherine, 1928.5
Recreation, 1965.1
Retton, Mary Lou, 1985.22
    and Olympic gold medal, 1985.24
Rice, Joan Moore, 1975.17

Title Index

199